lonely planet

Best Beaches
AUSTRALIA

100 of AUSTRALIA'S
MOST INCREDIBLE BEACHES

Contents

Queensland

New South Wales

Victoria

Tasmania

South Australia

Western Australia

Northern Territory

1. Whitehaven Beach
2. Little Cove
3. Burleigh Beach
4. Tangalooma Beach
5. Four Mile Beach
6. Seventy-Five Mile Beach
7. Lady Elliot Island
8. Horseshoe Bay
9. Nudey Beach
10. Rainbow Bay Beach
11. Langford Island Beach
12. Balding Bay
13. Surfers Paradise
14. Myall Beach
15. Low Isles/Wungkun
16. Mon Repos Beach
17. Sunset Beach
18. Yorke Island/Masig Beach
19. Bondi Beach
20. Lagoon Beach
21. Zenith Beach
22. Broken Head Beach
23. Camp Cove
24. Manly Beach
25. Pebbly Beach
26. Merewether Beach
27. Maitland Bay Beach
28. Hyams Beach
29. Crescent Head
30. Palm Beach
31. The Pass
32. Wattamolla Beach
33. Cabarita Beach
34. Emily Bay
35. Reef Beach
36. Number One Beach
37. Pambula River Mouth Beach
38. Balmoral Beach
39. Honeymoon Bay
40. North Smoky Beach
41. Ned's Beach
42. Bells Beach
43. Childers Cove
44. Squeaky Beach
45. Mount Martha Beach
46. Wreck Beach
47. Sorrento Ocean Beach
48. Ninety Mile Beach
49. Smiths Beach
50. Thurra Beach
51. Blanket Bay
52. Eastern Beach Reserve
53. Wineglass Bay
54. Fortescue Bay Beach
55. Binalong Bay
56. Hopground Beach
57. Disappointment Bay
58. Trousers Point Beach
59. The Neck
60. Boat Harbour Beach
61. South Cape Bay
62. Landing Beach
63. Seal Bay
64. Salmon Hole
65. Stokes Bay
66. Seacliff Beach
67. Almonta Beach
68. Vivonne Bay
69. Long Beach
70. Greenly Beach
71. Port Willunga Beach
72. Dolphin Beach
73. Ocean Beach
74. Stony Point Beach
75. Elephant Rocks
76. Lucky Bay
77. The Basin
78. Roebuck Bay
79. Meelup Beach
80. Cossies Beach
81. Hamelin Bay
82. Wharton Beach
83. Turquoise Bay
84. Misery Beach
85. Hellfire Bay
86. Cape Leveque/Kooljaman
87. Cottesloe Beach/Mudurup
88. Dolly Beach
89. Little Salmon Bay
90. Cable Beach/Walmanyjun
91. Monkey Mia Beach
92. Injidup Beach

93. James Price Point/Walmadan
94. Turtle Bay
95. Mindil Beach
96. Ngalarrkpuy/Lonely Beach
97. Galuru/East Woody Beach
98. Bremer Island/Dhambaliya
99. Barinura/Little Bondi Beach
100. Cobourg Coastal Camp Beach

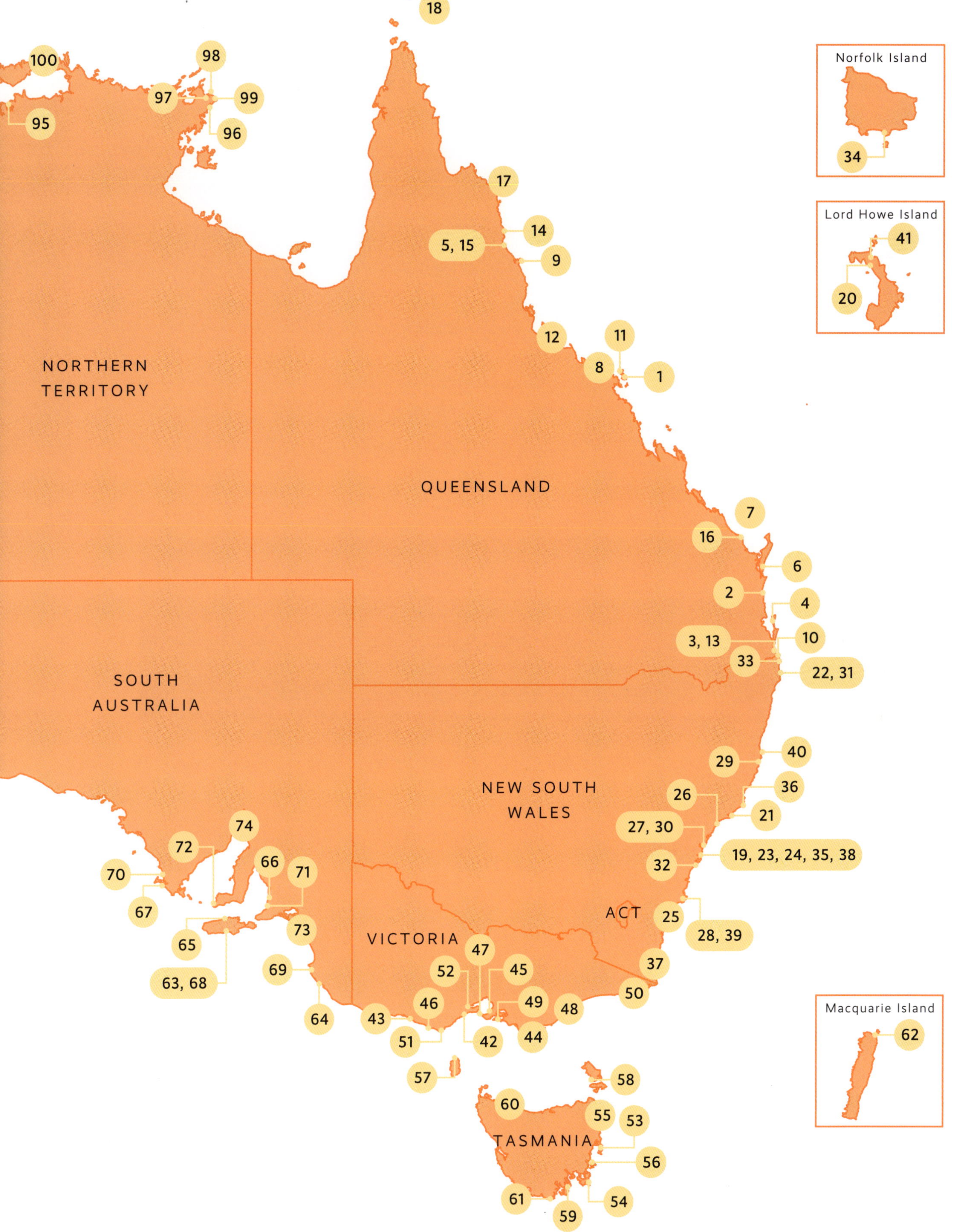

NORTHERN TERRITORY
QUEENSLAND
SOUTH AUSTRALIA
NEW SOUTH WALES
ACT
VICTORIA
TASMANIA
Norfolk Island
Lord Howe Island
Macquarie Island
100
98
97
99
95
96
18
17
14
5, 15
9
12
11
8
1
7
16
6
2
4
3, 13
10
33
22, 31
40
29
36
26
21
27, 30
19, 23, 24, 35, 38
32
25
28, 39
37
50
34
41
20
62
74
72
66
71
70
67
65
73
63, 68
69
64
47
52
45
46
49
48
43
51
42
44
57
58
60
55
53
56
61
59
54

Ready to Hit the Beach?

From Sydney's world-famous Bondi Beach to the blissfully undeveloped hidden coves of coastal national parks, Australia's beaches are legendary. There are more than 10,000 stretches of sand to explore Down Under, and they are among the cleanest and clearest in the world. Better yet, Australia doesn't have private beaches, so they are free for the public to use.

With such a rich collection to choose from, no two shortlists will ever be the same. For this book, our writers scoured thousands of kilometres of coastline to unearth 100 incredible beaches that showcase the mesmerising – and often surprising – diversity of Australia's beaches, from remote seaside idylls where you can pitch a tent to offshore-island gems, and sparkling urban beaches with accessibility infrastructure to help more people enjoy them. Slip into your swimwear and discover your new favourite stretch of sand. — *SARAH REID*

CULTURAL ICONS

Places for recreation, sport, cultural expression and wellbeing, beaches are integral to the Australian way of life. Growing up within cooee of the coast myself – as 87% of the population does today – my local beaches were my playgrounds, classrooms, social arenas and sanctuaries wrapped into one. Australian beaches continue to play those roles in my life today.

Australia's beaches are also important to coastal Aboriginal and Torres Strait Islander groups, who have lived in sync with their Sea Country for millennia. Look carefully, and you might spot cultural living sites – from sophisticated fish traps to remnants of ancient seafood feasts – hiding in plain sight. Public access is restricted at some places to protect this rich cultural heritage.

WILDLIFE MAGNETS

Australia's marine biodiversity is similarly rich. Whether you snorkel off a beach in South Australia or around a Great Barrier Reef island, there are myriad species to spot. You don't even need to get wet to meet some of the majestic marine creatures that frequent Australia's beaches, with dolphins, seabirds and migrating whales easily spotted from shore on the east and west coasts. Six of the world's seven turtle species nest on Australian beaches, and kangaroos can be spotted grazing near the seaside in many locations.

STAYING SAFE

Australia's beaches are as unpredictable as they are beautiful. Stay safe and swim between the red-and-yellow flags at beaches patrolled by professional lifeguards or volunteer lifesavers, and always assess your ability to cope with ocean conditions before entering the water. Shield yourself from the harsh Australian sun with SPF50+ sunscreen and protective clothing, and heed safety signage, from crocodile and stinger warnings in northern Australia to hazardous surf warnings anywhere.

ETIQUETTE

Australians value their personal space, and this extends to the beach. If there's room to spread out on the sand, use it, and avoid smoking – which is banned on many beaches – or making excessive noise, including playing music, near other beachgoers. Surf etiquette is paramount: don't drop in (take off in front of someone already on a wave) or snake (paddle around someone to catch a wave), know your limits, and wear a leash. And leave nothing behind on the sand but footprints to help ensure future generations can enjoy Australia's beaches just as much as we do today.

Top 5 Best Beaches for...

Mark Fitz
@_markfitz

Wildlife Watching

'From 'roos lazing on the sand to dolphins carving up the waves, Aussie beaches are wildlife magnets.'

SEAL BAY, 174
Kangaroo Island, South Australia

MON REPOS BEACH, 52
Bundaberg, Queensland

NED'S BEACH, 114
Lord Howe Island, New South Wales

THE BASIN, 206
Rottnest Island/Wadjemup, Western Australia

PEBBLY BEACH, 76
Murramarang National Park, New South Wales

Julie Jones
@havewheelchairwilltravel

Accessibility

'While Australia's beaches are lovely to look at, it's even better when everyone has access to get the sand between their toes.'

BONDI BEACH, 61
Sydney, New South Wales

FOUR MILE BEACH, 24
Port Douglas, Queensland

MONKEY MIA BEACH, 242
Shark Bay/Gutharraguda, Western Australia

MOUNT MARTHA BEACH, 128
Mornington Peninsula, Victoria

BURLEIGH BEACH, 19
Burleigh Heads, Gold Coast, Queensland

Jarryd & Alesha
@nomadasaurus

Snorkelling

'With over 34,000km of coastline and some of the most diverse marine and coral life on the planet, Australia is a snorkeller's paradise.'

LADY ELLIOT ISLAND, 28
Southern Great Barrier Reef, Queensland

NED'S BEACH, 114
Lord Howe Island, New South Wales

STONY POINT BEACH, 198
Whyalla, South Australia

TURQUOISE BAY, 221
Ningaloo/Nyinggulu Coast, Western Australia

MANLY BEACH, 72
Sydney/Warrane, New South Wales

Libby & Jamie
@out.here.exploring

Remote Beaches

'We love Australia's remote beaches for the unknown – the thrill of discovering the next hidden gem keeps us coming back for more.'

GREENLY BEACH, 190
Coulta, South Australia

TURQUOISE BAY, 221
Ningaloo/Nyinggulu Coast, Western Australia

HELLFIRE BAY, 224
Cape Le Grand National Park, Western Australia

SEVENTY-FIVE MILE BEACH, 26
Great Sandy National Park, K'gari, Queensland

DOLPHIN BEACH, 194
Dhilba Guuranda-Innes National Park, Yorke Peninsula, South Australia

Top 5 Best Beaches for...

Megsy & Family
@traveltales

Families

'We love beach-hopping along the Aussie coast and watching the kids grow more confident in the surf as they adapt to the unpredictability of the ocean.'

LUCKY BAY, 204
Cape Le Grand National Park, Western Australia

HYAMS BEACH, 82
Jervis Bay, New South Wales

WHITEHAVEN BEACH, 15
Whitsundays, Queensland

THE PASS, 91
Byron Bay, New South Wales

NINETY MILE BEACH, 136
East Gippsland, Victoria

Joss & Megan
@seaustravl

Camping

'Beach camping in Australia is pure freedom – waking up to the sound of waves, coffee in hand and the coastline as your backyard.'

BINALONG BAY, 155
Bay of Fires/Larapuna, Tasmania/Lutruwita

JAMES PRICE POINT/WALMADAN, 246
Broome/Rubibi, Western Australia

LUCKY BAY, 204
Cape Le Grand National Park, Western Australia

SQUEAKY BEACH, 126
West Gippsland, Victoria

SEVENTY-FIVE MILE BEACH, 26
Great Sandy National Park, K'gari, Queensland

Molly Picklum

@picklummolly

Surfing

'I've been lucky to surf all over the world, but nothing beats paddling out at an Aussie beach.'

Sarah Reid

@sarahreidtravels

Bushwalking

'Trails fringing Australia's best beaches offer yet another memorable way to immerse yourself in the nation's sublime coastal scenery.'

Queensland

ABOVE Tangalooma Bay
RIGHT Surfers Paradise

Whitehaven Beach

WHITSUNDAY ISLAND, WHITSUNDAYS

THE SWIRLING PATTERN of aquamarine water and snow-white sandbars at the northern end of Whitehaven Beach – officially called Hill Inlet – is one of Australia's most photogenic natural icons. And when you sink your toes into the 98% pure silica sands (its origin continues to baffle geologists) of this bewitching beach in Queensland's Whitsunday Islands National Park, you'll understand the hype. Framed by the shimmering Coral Sea and the lush vegetation of uninhabited Whitsunday Island, the 7km-long (4.3-mile) beach on the traditional lands of the Ngaro people is pure magic. Most day trips from neighbouring Hamilton Island and the mainland tourism hub of Airlie Beach include stops at Whitehaven Beach and the northern side of Hill Inlet, where you can (and should) take a 1.3km (0.8-mile) -return bushwalk to lookouts for mesmerising views before diving into Whitehaven's crystal-clear waters.

GETTING THERE

Whitehaven Beach is a 30-minute catamaran ride from Hamilton Island, and about one hour on a high-speed boat from Airlie Beach. Helicopter and seaplane tours are available for those in search of the perfect aerial shot. Boats are permitted to anchor in Hill Inlet and off Whitehaven Beach, and there's a basic national park campground at the southern end of the beach.

Little Cove

NOOSA HEADS, SUNSHINE COAST

AT THE NORTHERN TIP of Queensland's Sunshine Coast, Noosa Heads is legendary among longboarders for its quintet of right-hand point breaks that consistently break at the same speed and line. When the wind is blowing from the south and the swell rolls in from the north, that's when you want to paddle out at Noosa.

Noosa Heads' Main Beach is the most accessible for surfers and beachgoers, but it's only a 300m (984ft) stroll around the headland to Little Cove, which doesn't just have a great wave,

but also a lovely little slice of beach. Hugged by greenery, it feels much further from the tourist hub of Hastings St than it actually is. And while it's not patrolled, Little Cove is considered a safe spot for swimming.

Just beyond the northern end of the beach, the national park car park doubles as a trailhead for coastal wilderness walks, including the popular 10.8km (6.7-mile) return Coastal Walk, which takes you past Noosa's three other point breaks: Boiling Pot, Tea Tree Bay and Granite Bay.

GETTING THERE

Noosa Heads is 148km (92 miles) or about a two-hour drive north of Brisbane. With limited parking at Little Cove, you may have more luck finding a spot in town.

Burleigh Beach

BURLEIGH HEADS, GOLD COAST

LONG BEFORE THE SUPERBANK was created further south at Snapper Rocks (p36), there was one wave to rule them all on Queensland's Gold Coast: Burleigh Point. Surfers travelled from far and wide to slice up this right-hand point break, with the annual Stubbies Surf Classic held in the 1970s and '80s drawing thousands to watch top surfers in action, including locals Wayne 'Rabbit' Bartholomew and the late Micheal Peterson.

Burleigh remains one of the city's most popular beaches for surfers and swimmers, with its long, wide lick of blond sand offering plenty of space to roll out your towel, and a lifeguard tower staffed daily. Burleigh Point is one of the Gold Coast's more consistent waves, with offshore winds from the southwest combined with a moderate southeast swell offering the best conditions. Take care of rips and rocks, and expect crowds.

At the southern end of the beach, Burleigh Pavilion delivers a front-row seat to the surf from its drinking and dining venues, as well as sublime views towards the Surfers Paradise skyline to the north. Beach wheelchairs can be borrowed from the Burleigh Heads Mowbray Park Surf Life Saving Club on weekends from September to May (call ahead) or you can borrow one any day as part of a lockbox pilot program; visit the City of Gold Coast website for details.

Enjoy great views of the surf from the walking tracks lacing the 27-hectare (66.7-acre) headland rising up behind the beach, protected by Burleigh Heads National Park. Known to the Yugambeh people as Jellurgal, it's home to numerous sacred sites, including a 4000-year-old shell midden. Follow the Ocean View Track from the Pavilion around the headland to the Jellurgal Aboriginal Cultural Centre to learn more about the headland's rich cultural heritage.

GETTING THERE

Burleigh lies 11km (7 miles) north of Gold Coast Airport, with taxis, rideshares and shuttles available. From 2026, an extension of the Gold Coast Light Rail links Broadbeach South to Burleigh Heads in about 16 minutes. Beachfront parking is also available.

The trail will also take you alongside the crystal-clear Tallebudgera Creek, which separates the headland from Palm Beach to the south. The calm waters and sandy beaches lining the creek are popular with families and present an ideal refuge when northerly and easterly winds lash Burleigh Beach. Look closely and you might see the historic Aboriginal fish trap hiding in the shallows near Tallebudgera Creek Bridge.

Tangalooma Beach

MORETON ISLAND/MULGUMPIN

THE WORLD'S THIRD-LARGEST SAND ISLAND, Moreton Island/ Mulgumpin is an idyll of blond sandy beaches, rolling dunes, native bushland and serene lagoons some 57km (35 miles) off the coast of Brisbane/Meanjin. With 95% of the isle protected by the Gheebulum Kunungai (Moreton Island) National Park and Moreton Island Recreation Area, it's a sublime spot to unplug by the sea near Queensland's capital.

A thin ribbon of white sand backed by coastal scrub winds along the island's protected west coast. Roughly in the middle, the section known as Tangalooma is famous for its 15 wrecks scuttled just offshore (1963–84) to create a safe anchorage. Now encrusted with corals and swarming with fish, it's a popular snorkelling spot – Tangalooma means 'where fish gather' in the language of the island's Quandamooka Traditional Custodians. Rays, dolphins, wobbegong sharks, turtles and elusive dugongs are also seen here.

There's a campsite tucked behind the beach; you'll need 4WD to access campgrounds beyond Tangalooma, as the island's 'roads' are sand tracks.

GETTING THERE

Four daily passenger ferry services (75 minutes) depart from Holt Street Wharf in Pinkenba, Brisbane, and arrive at the Tangalooma Jetty on Moreton Island. A car ferry runs on a demand-based schedule from the Port of Brisbane. Or visit on a day cruise from Brisbane.

Four Mile Beach

PORT DOUGLAS

WITH AN UNRULY STRIP of palm-studded rainforest skirting its golden sands, it's hard to believe that Four Mile Beach lies just steps from the centre of the Tropical North Queensland resort town of Port Douglas. Stretching for 4km (2.5 miles), it delivers a remote-tropical-beach experience with urban amenities. The northern end is patrolled, with a netted swimming enclosure erected here during the deadly marine stinger season (November to May). Saltwater crocodiles are occasionally spotted at Four Mile, making another great case for paddling in sight of the lifeguard

tower, where a beach wheelchair and matting is available.

A magical time to visit this beach on the traditional lands of the Eastern Kuku Yalanji and Yirrganydji peoples is just before sunrise, when the sky morphs from pink to gold as the sun peeks above the Coral Sea. It's a popular time for locals to walk their dogs, with an off-leash area at the southern end of the beach. Hike up the Flagstaff Hill Walking Trail at the northern tip for post-card-perfect views from the lookout along the sand.

GETTING THERE

Port Douglas is 67km (42 miles) or just over a one-hour drive north of Cairns/Gimuy.

Seventy-Five Mile Beach

GREAT SANDY NATIONAL PARK, K'GARI

SPANNING THE ENTIRE EAST COAST of the island national park of K'gari (formerly Fraser Island), 75 Mile Beach is one of Queensland's wildest coastal frontiers. Stretching over 120km (75 miles), it's a sand highway, a living museum, a free-range zoo and a beach-fisher and camper's nirvana rolled into one. Most visitors begin their K'gari adventure at its southern tip. Look out for wild dingoes as you drive north (4WD essential) along the honeycomb-hued beach in search of attractions, such as the rusting wreck of the SS *Maheno*, washed ashore in 1935 near a collection of unusual sand dunes known as the Pinnacles.

Unpredictable ocean currents and marine life make the freshwater Eli Creek and the natural rock pools (the Champagne Pools) the safest spots for a swim, and with nine camping zones, there is no shortage of scenic spots to pitch a tent. Respect the island's Butchulla Traditional Custodians – and the next island visitors – and leave no trace of your adventure.

GETTING THERE

A car ferry shuttles between Inskip Point and the southern tip of K'gari from 6am to 5pm daily (10 minutes). Another car ferry makes three daily trips between River Heads, just south of Hervey Bay, and Kingfisher Bay Resort on K'gari's west coast.

Lady Elliot Island

SOUTHERN GREAT BARRIER REEF

FEW ISLANDS HAVE A COMEBACK STORY quite like this remote coral cay at the southern tip of Queensland's Great Barrier Reef. Stripped almost bare by guano miners in the late 1800s, with new growth prevented by goats placed on the island to ensure food for shipwrecked seafarers, Lady Elliot Island had been reduced to little more than a field of compacted coral by the mid-20th century.

A small resort was opened on the degraded island in 1969 and a DIY revegetation programme commenced. But it wasn't until Peter Gash, Lady Elliot's current custodian, took over in 2005 that the regeneration of the island shifted into high gear. Its forest ecosystem has since been largely restored, providing a haven for seabirds and even marine life as nutrients seep through the 'beach rock' and fertilise the fringing reef. Run almost entirely on renewable energy, the island's low-key eco-resort has a minimal effect on this rich habitat.

One of the best ways to enjoy the 42-hectare (104-acre) island is to walk around the crushed coral and sand beach encircling it, which takes about 45 minutes without stops. The eco-resort is located on the east-facing 'sunrise' side of the island, where a shallow reef stretches towards the horizon, and durable plastic sunloungers provide a comfortable seat for quiet contemplation as the sun rises above the Coral Sea. You can only snorkel here at high tide, when you're likely to meet a few turtles. Can you hear that crackling sound? It's a sign of a healthy reef.

Head clockwise around the island and look out for rare red-tailed tropicbirds nesting under the octopus bushes lining the shore. As you round the southwestern corner of the island, see its 1893 lighthouse towering over the west-facing 'sunset' beach. This part of the beach is a launchpad for snorkelling and diving adventures in deeper waters, with mere steps separating you from your next manta ray encounter. As the sun begins its evening descent, overnight guests gather here to watch the sky light up with a cool drink in-hand and the sand between their toes.

GETTING THERE

Lady Elliot Island is only accessible by a small aircraft flight from Bundaberg, Hervey Bay, Brisbane, or the Gold Coast, arranged by Lady Elliot Island Eco Resort as part of your visit. Day trips are possible, but a longer stay is recommended to enjoy the island to the fullest.

Horseshoe Bay

BOWEN

THE HOME OF THE RICH AND JUICY Kensington Pride mango, the coastal town of Bowen at the northern end of the Whitsundays region also lays claim to one of Australia's prettiest beaches. Framed by headlands of rounded granite boulders, the 150m-long (494ft) cove of Horseshoe Bay is patrolled on weekends and school holidays during the warmer months. There's decent snorkelling around the beach's headlands and fringing reef. Don't miss *Bywa,* an underwater sculpture by Torres Strait Islander artist Brian Robinson, which takes its name from a word

in the Kala Lagaw Ya dialect of the Western Islands of Torres Strait meaning 'waterspout'. Located on the traditional lands of the Juru Aboriginal people, Bowen also has rich Torres Strait Islander and South Sea Islander heritage.

Take a 10-minute hike up to the Rotary Lookout for superb views over the beach and discover more beautiful Bowen bays on the 2.5km (1.6-mile) Cape Edgecumbe Walking Trail linking Horseshoe Bay with Murray and Rose bays. Allow an hour for the return walk.

GETTING THERE

Horseshoe Bay is 4km (2.5 miles) from Bowen's town centre and 84km (52 miles) or an hour's drive north of Whitsunday Coast Airport.

Nudey Beach

FITZROY ISLAND, CAIRNS REGION

IT MIGHT SURPRISE FIRST-TIME VISITORS to this Great Barrier Reef gateway hub to discover that Cairns/Gimuy is not a beach destination – its muddy foreshore is more popular with coastal birds. But with Fitzroy Island on its doorstep, it doesn't need to be.

Before sea levels rose around 9500 years ago, Aboriginal groups could walk to this small, hilly island 5km (3 miles) from the mainland to fish, gather food, and hold ceremonies. Now a national park, Fitzroy Island offers a classic tropical-island experience just 45 minutes from Cairns.

Ferries arrive at Welcome Bay, where a 1.2km (0.75-mile) return shaded rainforest track leads to small, undeveloped Nudey Beach which, despite its name, isn't clothing-optional. Bookended by granite boulders, with turquoise water lapping its crunchy white-coral sand, the setting is sublime. There's good snorkelling off the northern end of the beach, with pretty patches of hard and soft corals visited by angelfish, butterflyfish, parrotfish and wrasses, along with the odd green turtle.

GETTING THERE

The *Fitzroy Flyer* ferry runs three daily services between Cairns and Fitzroy Island in both directions. There is a resort with two restaurants and a campground on the island.

Rainbow Bay Beach

COOLANGATTA,
GOLD COAST

WHEN THE SWELL, WIND AND TIDE ALIGN, the eyes of the surfing world turn to the Superbank at the southern tip of the Gold Coast. Formed by a combination of natural processes and human intervention, the long sandbank stretching between Snapper Rocks and Kirra Beach has produced perfect hollow barrels in the right conditions since 2002.

For first dibs on the turquoise tubes, Rainbow Bay Beach, closest to the Snapper Rocks headland, is the place to paddle out – or spectate from its golden sands. Time your visit with the World Surf League Championship Tour in May, and you can watch the globe's best surfers in action. You can also watch talented surfers tear up the waves from the elevated restaurant and bar at Rainbow Bay Surf Life Saving Club on the foreshore.

Follow the path around the headland to the fingernail of sand known as Froggies Beach, Queensland's southernmost beach, or head down to Kirra's smaller swells for more beginner-friendly waves.

GETTING THERE

Rainbow Bay Beach is 4km (2.5 miles) from Gold Coast Airport and 32km (20 miles) from Broadbeach, at the heart of the Gold Coast. From Broadbeach you can catch bus number 700 to Coolangatta (allow an hour).

Langford Island Beach

WHITSUNDAYS

WHITEHAVEN BEACH GETS ALL THE GLORY, but there are plenty of other beautiful beaches fringing the 74 islands of the Whitsundays. A lesser-known highlight is the ribbon of ivory sand stretching nearly a kilometre from the southeastern tip of Langford Island into the shallow aqua waters of Langford-Bird Reef. Visit at low tide to walk its length before your tracks are submerged by the incoming tide.

The best snorkelling is on the northern side of the small, uninhabited island, where you're likely to spot green turtles along with reef fish aplenty as you float over colourful coral gardens. Lined by native bottle trees that burst into bloom in spring, a short path from the base of the island leads to a lookout for serene views of the sand spit and surrounding islands.

GETTING THERE

Langford Island can be visited on boat tours from neighbouring Hayman Island (just seven minutes away) or mainland Airlie Beach, 26km (16 miles) to the southwest. Or you can charter a boat in Airlie and sail here yourself – no boat licence required. Camping and mooring overnight at Langford Island overnight are not permitted.

Balding Bay

MAGNETIC ISLAND/YUNBENUN

QUEENSLAND MAY BE the only Australian state or territory lacking an official nudist beach, but that doesn't stop locals and visitors to Magnetic Island's Balding Bay (Yunbenun to its Traditional Wulgurukaba Custodians) from getting their kit off here.

It takes a bit of effort to get to the state's best-known unofficial nudist beach – the 2.8km (1.7-mile) return track from neighbouring Horseshoe Bay is very steep with many steps; sturdy footwear is recommended. But it's all part of the experience – keep an eye out for orange-flanked rainbow skinks basking on the rocky path.

Upon reaching the remote-feeling bay, where a small arc of golden sand settles between granite-boulder headlands, diving into the tropical water is *de rigueur*, clothed or not (outside the November to May stinger season). While the Great Barrier Reef protects Balding Bay from powerful waves, be mindful that help is at least a 40-minute hike away.

GETTING THERE

Magnetic Island is a 20- to 40-minute ferry ride from Townsville. Bring your car or e-bike, or take a bus from the Nelly Bay ferry dock to Horseshoe Bay (p32), 7km (4.5 miles). The track to Balding Bay begins at the eastern end of Horseshoe Bay.

Surfers Paradise

GOLD COAST

SURFERS PARADISE, on southeastern Queensland's Gold Coast, is quite unlike any other beach in Australia – and proud to be. A sublime 2km (1.2-mile) strip of sand wedged between the blue Pacific Ocean on one side and a skyscraper skyline on the other, it's a shimmering monument to everything money can buy. It's dominated by Australia's tallest building, Q1, which has an observation deck 230m (754.6ft) above beach level, offering views as far south as Byron Bay in Northern NSW.

It's also glitzy and brash, a sort of Vegas-by-the-sea, where you can party all night and recover the next day with a kebab and a dip in the surf. For decades, starting in 1964, Surfers Paradise's reputation for cheeky glamour was personified by 'meter maids' in gold bikinis and tiaras (later Akubra hats), who would walk the Esplanade topping up parking meters to encourage visitors to stay. When the meters were automated, the meter maids were so synonymous with Surfers they stayed, and can still be seen posing for photos with tourists.

Even the name 'Surfers Paradise' was a marketing idea. The demurely named beachside suburb of Elston was renamed in 1933 after the Surfers Paradise Hotel that had just been built by Brisbane hotelier Jim Cavill. His name now graces the pedestrian mall that's the buzzing epicentre of Surfers, lined with surf shops, tattoo parlours, fast-food joints and nightclubs.

GETTING THERE

Surfers Paradise is 77km (48 miles) from Brisbane/Meanjin and 28km (17.5 miles) north of Gold Coast Airport. Parking can be limited, but there are combined train and tram options from Brisbane. Try to avoid Schoolies Week in late November and early December, when Surfers is inundated by up to 40,000 high-school graduates from all over Australia.

All of which only seems to enhance the natural beauty of this long beach. When the conditions are right, it lives up to its name as a paradise for surfers, although breaks such as Kirra and Snapper Rocks further south tend to get more consistent waves. Being such an open beach, Surfers is prone to rips and other dangerous currents – but it's also one of the safest beaches in Australia, with three lifeguard towers, year-round patrols and a surf club that celebrated its 100th anniversary in 2025. And in the afternoon, when the apartment blocks and high-rise hotels cast their long shadows across the sand, you're somewhat safer from sunburn.

Myall Beach

DAINTREE NATIONAL PARK, CAPE TRIBULATION/KULKI

GNARLED COCONUT PALMS bend over the pearly sands of Cape Tribulation/Kulki, holding back the Daintree Rainforest from spilling into the calm, turquoise waters of the Coral Sea. Stretching southward from this remote, Tropical North Queensland headland, east-facing Myall Beach is a perfect example of the otherworldly coastal beauty of this wild corner of Australia, stewarded by the Eastern Kuku Yalanji people for millennia.

The ever-present risk of saltwater crocodiles makes this a beach for strolling rather than swimming. And what a spot for a wild walk; especially when the first rays of the morning sun unfurl across the ocean, and the world's oldest living tropical lowland rainforest erupts with birdsong. Plus, with half-day Great Barrier Reef snorkelling trips operating daily from this very beach, you can get wet safely just 25 minutes offshore.

GETTING THERE

Myall Beach is 140km (87 miles) or a 2.5-hour drive north of Cairns/Gimuy. The beach can be accessed at two points: via a 350m (1148ft) walking track from the Kulki day-use area or a 370m (1214ft) walking track from the Dubuji day-use area. Or take the wheelchair-accessible Dubuji boardwalk through the forest for 1.2km (0.75 miles).

Low Isles/ Wungkun

PORT DOUGLAS

CAPTAIN COOK'S LOG described the 'small low island' he sighted from the Endeavour on 10 June, 1770, and set about giving it an unimaginative renaming. In reality, the Low Isles off Port Douglas have been known to the Eastern Kuku Yalanji and Yirrganydji peoples for centuries as Wungkun, an important cultural site and Dreaming place.

A teardrop of sun-kissed sand with an 1878 lighthouse rising above a cluster of palm and casuarina trees, the smaller of the two coral cays that comprise the Low Isles was made for a day on the beach. A string of permanent umbrellas provides much-needed shade on sultry Tropical North Queensland days, and a reef – part of the Great Barrier Reef Marine Park – begins just steps from the shore. There are 150 corals for snorkellers to count, along with turtles, reef sharks and a cornucopia of tropical fish. Not just a pretty reef, this rich marine ecosystem has played an important role in global reef science. The world's first scientific study of a coral reef was undertaken here in 1928, with subsequent studies helping scientists understand how reef systems decline, recover and change over long periods of time.

GETTING THERE

Port Douglas is 67km (41.5 miles) from Cairns/Gimuy, which has an international airport. Port Douglas-based operators offer a variety of Low Isles tour options, from speedboat snorkelling tours that return to you the marina in less than 2.5 hours, to leisurely catamaran sojourns.

With boat tours from Port Douglas taking as little as 15 minutes to make the 15km (9.3-mile) journey to the island, it's perfect for visitors looking for a taste of the Great Barrier Reef but lacking the time for a full-day trip to the outer reef. Visit on a calm, sunny day for the best snorkelling conditions, ideally at high tide, and don't stress about crocodiles, with only three glimpsed out here in as nearly as many decades. Not much of a snorkeller? You can circumnavigate the 1.6-hectare (4-acre) island in as few as 15 minutes.

Automated in 1993, the island's lighthouse no longer requires a keeper, but the Great Barrier Reef Marine Park Authority (GBMPA) appoints a new set of caretakers roughly every two years to ensure the Low Isles' natural and heritage values are maintained. If this sounds like your dream job, keep an eye on GBMPA's Facebook page.

Mon Repos Beach

BUNDABERG

BACKED BY PANDANUS AND SHE-OAK TREES, the generous sweep of golden sand known as Mon Repos looks like many other beaches in the Bundaberg region at the gateway to the Southern Great Barrier Reef. Yet its significance cannot be understated. A culturally important place for four identified Aboriginal groups – Taribelang Bunda, Gooreng Gooreng, Gurang, and Byellee peoples – Mon Repos also supports the largest concentration of nesting marine turtles on the eastern Australian mainland.

Between November and January, more than 300 turtles – mostly endangered loggerheads – heave themselves up onto the dunes of Mon Repos to lay their eggs. Six to eight weeks later (typically between January to March), thousands of hatchlings emerge and scuttle down to the sea. This incredible spectacle can be witnessed on a ranger-led Turtle Encounter held nightly during turtle season, with beach wheelchair access possible with support people. The excellent wheelchair-accessible Mon Repos Turtle Centre is open year-round. Swim with care at this unpatrolled beach.

GETTING THERE

Mon Repos Beach is 14km (9 miles) or a 17-minute drive north-east of central Bundaberg. The beach and coastal walking tracks are closed annually between 6pm and 6am from 15 October to 31 May.

Sunset Beach

LIZARD ISLAND, NORTHERN GREAT BARRIER REEF

A COVE OF FINE SAND punctuated by smooth granite boulders perfect for lounging on like the island's namesake, Sunset Beach lies within the elegantly understated Lizard Island Resort. It's a beach for serenity, sea-swims and sundowners; and because it faces west, it's also sheltered from the easterly trade winds. To the Dingaal people, the island is Jiigurru ('stingray') because of its shape, but in 1770 Captain James Cook renamed it after the many lizards he saw while climbing to the island's highest point, 350m (1148ft) above sea level, in search of a safe passage through the surrounding reefs. Almost the entire island is national park, declared in 1937, and its waters, part of the Great Barrier Reef Marine Park, teem with an astounding 1600 species, including enigmatic dwarf minke whales and 400 kinds of hard corals. Marine biologists conduct vital research into the future of Australia's precious coral reefs from a research station near Sunset Beach, set up in 1973.

GETTING THERE

Lizard Island lies 27km (17 miles) off the coast of northern Queensland and 250km (155 miles) or a one-hour scenic flight north-east of Cairns/Gimuy. Charter vessels also visit the island from Cairns, Cooktown and Port Douglas. There's a BYO-everything national park campground at Watson's Bay.

Yorke Island/Masig

TORRES STRAIT ISLANDS

SOME OF AUSTRALIA'S MOST REMOTE BEACHES are found in the Torres Strait Islands, a necklace of more than 200 tropical islands strung between the tip of Queensland's Cape York Peninsula and Papua New Guinea. Just a short ferry ride from the mainland, the Inner Islands (particularly Thursday Island/Waiben and Horn Island/Ngurupai) are the easiest to visit, but the presence of crocodiles makes beachgoing a risky activity.

Up in the Central Islands, teardrop-shaped Yorke Island/Masig has the best of both worlds: a blinding white-sand beach dipped in cerulean water and a rich island culture to discover. Like all inhabited Torres Strait Islands beyond the Inner Islands, it requires special permission to visit and a series of expensive flights to reach. Local operator Strait Experience makes it a whole lot easier with its Coray Cays & Culture tour, which includes charter flights from Cairns/Gimuy and three days on the island, where you'll dive into its little-known history and culture as well as its beautiful beaches. While it's not a cheap trip, it's one of the most unique and enriching Australian beach experiences you'll find.

GETTING THERE

Strait Experience runs its three-day, two-night Coray Cays & Culture tour on demand.

New South Wales

LEFT The Pass
ABOVE Pebbly Beach

Bondi Beach

SYDNEY/WARRANE

SYNONYMOUS WITH SYDNEY/WARRANE, Bondi Beach is so much more than 1km (0.6 miles) of blond shore bookended by golden sandstone cliffs. It's a cultural icon – the birthplace of the world's first surf-lifesaving organisation, formed in 1907, and the setting of countless films and television series, including one of Australia's longest-running shows, *Bondi Rescue*.

The closest surf beach to the city centre (7km/4.5 miles away), Bondi has cerulean water and consistently surfable waves, particularly at the southern end. It hosts visitors from all corners of the city – and the world – particularly on summer weekends, when beachgoers descend in their thousands.

If the surf is too gnarly for you, head to the child-friendly ocean baths at either end of the beach. At the southern end, the turquoise Bondi Icebergs pool is as renowned as the beach itself, famous for its hardy locals who make their daily laps year-round as waves crash over the edge. The popular 6km (3.5-mile) clifftop Bondi-to-Coogee coastal walk also begins at the southern end of Bondi. Changing rooms and lockers can be found at the historic Bondi Pavilion in the middle of the park behind the beach, with beach wheelchairs available for use at the northern end of the promenade (contact Waverly Council to book), before the ramp. There's also a beach wheelchair-shower here, and accessible bathrooms in the pavilion.

GETTING THERE

Take a train to Bondi Junction and transfer to any bus bound for Bondi Beach. The combined journey from the city centre by public transport takes around 45 minutes. Limited parking is also available at the beachfront and on surrounding streets.

Looking for your LGBTIQ+ community? Head to North Bondi, where buff bods glisten in budgie smugglers (Speedos) and flex at the outdoor gym. There's also a grassy park with coin-operated barbecues, and if you wander further up the headland, near Bondi Golf and Diggers Club, you can admire Aboriginal rock engravings thought to have been carved by ancestors of the Bidjigal and Gadigal clans of the Eora Nation some 2000 years ago.

The installation of shark nets off Bondi Beach remains a controversial topic, with nets across New South Wales entangling hundreds of non-target species each year. Bondi hasn't experienced a fatal shark encounter since 1929; though in 2022, it hit the headlines following the first shark-related fatality in Sydney's Eastern Beaches in almost 60 years, 10km (6 miles) south of Bondi. You're much more likely to see bottlenose dolphins.

Lagoon Beach

LORD HOWE ISLAND

IF EVER A BEACH had an unfair advantage, it's Lagoon Beach, which lies on the western side of one of the most naturally beautiful islands in the world. But the lagoon in its name is the real star: 6km (3.5 miles) long and about 100m (328ft) wide, flanked by a sandy beach on one side and the world's most southerly coral reef on the other, with two Tahiti-like mountains at its southern end. It's basically a colossal outdoor swimming pool that does double duty as an open-air aquarium – for Lord Howe, often called 'the Galapagos of the Pacific', is home to more than 500 species of fish and 90 species of coral. And at the end of a day spent ocean swimming, snorkelling, stand-up paddleboarding, sea kayaking or surfing (on the edge of the reef), Lagoon Beach promises one more delight, because of its western orientation: golden sunsets, with mountain views, glimmering on the waters you've been immersed in all day.

GETTING THERE

Lord Howe Island lies almost 700km (435 miles) northeast of Sydney/Warrane, at the same latitude as Port Macquarie. There are daily flights to the island from Sydney and weekly flights from Newcastle, Port Macquarie and the Gold Coast.

Zenith Beach

PORT STEPHENS

SOAKING UP THE PANORAMIC coastal views from the 161m (528ft) summit of Tomaree Head is a quintessential Port Stephens experience. Directly below is one of several glorious beaches naturally carved from this rugged stretch of coastline north of Newcastle/Muloobinba, perfect for cooling off after the steep hike up Tomaree Head.

Framed by ancient volcanic headlands cloaked in the native forests of Tomaree National Park, unpatrolled Zenith Beach feels deceptively remote – Shoal Bay, the closest village, is less than 1km (0.6 miles) down the road. Just 120m (394ft) from the car park, its clear waters beckon confident swimmers and surfers, with June to August bringing the best waves and whale-watching opportunities. Dolphins are frequent visitors, and an array of birdlife can be seen here throughout the year. Zenith Beach also marks the beginning of the Tomaree Coastal Walk, a three-day, 27km (17-mile) walking adventure linking secluded beaches, coastal villages and koala habitats on Worimi traditional lands.

GETTING THERE

Zenith Beach is 220km (137 miles) or nearly three hours' drive north of Sydney/Warrane. The 130 bus from Newcastle to Fingal Head stops at Zenith Beach, via Nelson Bay.

Broken Head Beach

BROKEN HEAD NATURE RESERVE, NORTH COAST

THE LONG AND WILD beach stretching 7km (4.5 miles) south from the historic Cape Byron Lighthouse comes to a dramatic end at Broken Head Beach. Surrounded by the coastal rainforest of the Broken Head Nature Reserve, 'Broken' remains largely unchanged from the beach that road-tripping surfers 'discovered' in the 1960s; a small caravan park is the only beachside development and limited parking restricts crowds. A long, hollow right-hander peels around the rocky point in the right conditions (look for a southeasterly swell with a southwesterly offshore wind) and there are rock pools to discover at low tide.

Follow the 1.6km (1-mile) return Three Sisters Walking Track around the headland for glorious views and to learn about Broken's significance to its Arakwal Traditional Custodians. Known as the Three Sisters, the series of rocky outcrops rising from the water beyond the headland tell the story of three sisters turned to stone by their ancestors. They're a warning to future generations about the importance of respecting cultural traditions – and to take care at this beach patrolled only in the summer school holidays (late December through January).

GETTING THERE

Located on the New South Wales North Coast, Broken Head Beach is 9km (5.6 miles) or a 15-minute drive south of Byron Bay.

BERKELEY

Camp Cove

SYDNEY/WARRANE

IN 1788, THE FIRST FLEET sailed into this sheltered cove on the traditional lands of the Birrabirragal clan of the Eora Nation. It's thought Governor Arthur Philip first came ashore at this picturesque bay tucked inside South Head before the fleet officially landed at Sydney Cove, now known as Circular Quay. Just 220m (722ft) wide and lapped by blue, Mediterranean-like water, it's a gorgeous spot for a swim, with fabulous views of the city skyline from the sand.

At the northern end you'll see the tiny 1881 sandstone cottage designed by prominent colonial architect John Kirkpatrick to house one of the southern hemisphere's first marine-biology research stations. From here, follow the 1km (0.6-mile) South Head Heritage Trail, which takes you along a cobblestone road past Lady Bay Beach (a designated nude beach) before reaching the distinctive, candy-striped Hornby Lighthouse. Note the historic cannon perched on the headland above Camp Cove en route.

GETTING THERE

Take a bus from Town Hall (about 50 minutes) to Camp Cove, or drive in half the time. The most scenic way to reach this beach is by ferry from Circular Quay to Watsons Bay, followed by a 600m (1968ft) walk, a 30-minute journey in total.

Manly Beach

SYDNEY/WARRANE

'SEVEN MILES FROM SYDNEY and a thousand miles from care.' Manly is a Sydney/Warrane suburb now, but this tagline for the steamship company that transported visitors to Manly in the 1870s still rings true, particularly when you step off the Manly Ferry into a sensory infusion of sunshine, salt air and seagulls.

Named by British admiral Arthur Phillip after the 'manly behaviour' of the Gayamaygal men his First Fleet crew encountered in 1788 at Manly Cove (originally Kai'ymay), Manly became one of Australia's most popular seaside resort towns in the late 19th and early 20th centuries. It's where a ban on daylight 'sea bathing' was first challenged, and lifted, in 1902. Soon afterwards, surf lifesaving began with the establishment of Manly Life Saving Club. And although surfing officially took off at neighbouring Freshwater Beach in the summer of 1914–15, when local teenager Isabel Letham went tandem-surfing with Hawaiian Olympian Duke Kahanamoku, it was Manly that hosted the first world surfing championship in 1964 (won by Midget Farrelly in front of 60,000 spectators). Both beaches now lie within the Manly Freshwater World Surfing Reserve, declared in 2012.

GETTING THERE

Manly is 17km (10.5 miles) north of Sydney's Central Business District (CBD) and best reached by ferry from Circular Quay, which takes 20 to 30 minutes. You can also get there by bus (from Wynyard Station) and car, but parking can be limited and expensive.

Manly's 2km (1.5-mile) strip of golden sand flanked by Norfolk Island pine trees and a wide beachside promenade is actually three beaches, each with its own vibe and surf-lifesaving club: Queenscliff, at the northern end, has its own ocean pool (and a secret tunnel through the rock to Freshwater); North Steyne is in the middle; and South Steyne occupies the sheltered southern corner.

Stroll along the coastal path from Manly Life Saving Club at South Steyne and you'll find a fourth Manly beach. Shelly Beach is a sheltered family-friendly spot – also popular with scuba divers and snorkellers, thanks to its abundant marine life, including gentle blue groupers. There's also the local 'Bold and Beautiful' swim squad (in bright pink caps) that tackles the 1.5km (1-mile) ocean swim from South Steyne to Shelly every morning. As if all that weren't enough, Manly has harbourside beaches too – secret sandy coves Little Manly, Delwood and Fairlight – some of which have their own ocean pools and swimming enclosures.

Pebbly Beach

MURRAMARANG NATIONAL PARK, SOUTH COAST

SECLUDED LOCATION, SOFT WHITE sand that squeals when you shuffle through it, clear blue water, surrounded by undeveloped Australian bush... Pebbly Beach ticks all the beautiful-beach boxes, with an added wildcard: its resident population of eastern grey kangaroos that lounge under the trees in the heat of the day, metres from the sea, nibbling the grass at dawn or dusk, joeys occasionally peeking from their mums' pouches to take in the beach views. What could be more Australian than a beach picnic surrounded by 'roos, followed by a dip in the ocean (being mindful of rips, particularly at either end of this unpatrolled beach). For surfers, the south-facing aspect means you're sheltered from the prevailing northerly winds. There's a kiosk (open on summer weekends) and a small campground with bush campsites and four simple beachside shacks, where you can wake to the morning melodies of whipbirds, wattlebirds and kookaburras.

GETTING THERE

Pebbly Beach is about 270km (168 miles) south of Sydney/Warrane. Turn off the Princes Hwy just south of Termeil and follow Pebbly Beach Rd for 8km (5 miles) through Murramarang National Park. Pebbly Beach is also on the three-day, 34km (21-mile) Murramarang South Coast Walk between Pretty Beach and Batemans Bay.

Merewether Beach

NEWCASTLE

THE TRAINING GROUND OF MANY SURFING LEGENDS, including four-time surfing world champion, Mark 'MR' Richards, Merewether Beach's unique combination of rock shelves and reefs mean it can be surfed at any time, on any tide, and in any swell, wind or size. Designated a National Surfing Reserve in 2009, Merewether is also the home of Surfest, Australia's largest surfing festival, held across February and March.

Before the first surfers paddled out here in the 1950s, Merewether was a favourite campsite of the Awabakal people, who still use the area today for cultural teachings and gathering traditional resources, such as ochre. The southern hemisphere's largest ocean pool was chipped out of the rocky shoreline in 1935, with 10 unroped lap lanes in the deeper of its two 50m (164ft) pools; both have ramp access. A series of rock pools offer additional spots for a safe splash, while a sandy stretch north of the rocks has easy access to the surf, with lifeguards or surf lifesavers on duty year-round. Overlooking the sand, the Merewether Surfhouse provides a superb vantage point.

GETTING THERE

Merewether Beach is 3.5km (2 miles) southwest of central Newcastle. Buses run here, or allow 45 minutes on foot.

Maitland Bay Beach

BOUDI NATIONAL PARK, CENTRAL COAST

THE IRON PADDLE STEAMER *MAITLAND* set off from Sydney at 11pm on 5 May, 1898, with the view of arriving in Newcastle by 9am the following morning, but it never made it. Its tragic wreck at Bouddi Point was so significant that the adjacent beach (where survivors landed) was named after it. The remains of the ship can still be seen at low tide at the eastern end of the golden bay, reached by a winding 1km (0.6-mile) bushwalk through Bouddi National Park on the traditional lands of the Darkinjung people. The walk itself is beautiful, but the undeveloped beach at the end is pure bliss, especially when offshore winds turn the cobalt bay to glass.

The beach is also accessible via the clifftop Bouddi Coastal Walk, a spectacular 8.5km (5.5-mile) one-way trail linking Killcare's Putty Beach to MacMasters Beach at the northern end of the national park. Even if you're not walking its entire length, it's worth following the trail from the eastern end of the beach up to Tooron-gong Lookout for a great vantage point.

GETTING THERE

The Maitland Bay Walking Track begins at the Maitland Bay Visitor Centre on Scenic Rd, Killcare Heights (20km or 12.5 miles from Gosford), which has a car park.

Hyams Beach

JERVIS BAY

IT'S OFTEN WRONGLY DESCRIBED as having the world's whitest sand (a 2006 study found Western Australia's Lucky Bay to be even whiter), but there's no denying that Hyams Beach is as white as the waters of the vast Jervis Bay are blue.

The contrast between its snow-white sand and the over-exposed gradient of blue water darkening into the depths made Hyams so social-media famous that in 2019 the local Shoalhaven council appointed traffic controllers to redirect visitors from the

tiny Hyams beach village. As you may have guessed, this is a beach best avoided during the summer (and autumn and spring) school holidays, especially weekends. Aim for a windless, off-season weekday, and you won't just have a better chance at scoring a parking spot – Hyams' dreamy blues will beam you straight to heaven on Earth. Bring a snorkel and look for groupers and stingrays at the northern end of the beach, known as Little Hyams.

GETTING THERE

Hyams Beach is 200km (124 miles) or around three hours' drive south of Sydney/Warrane. Park at Greenfield Beach and take the White Sands Walk (1.7km/1 mile) to Hyams Beach, which takes you past the similarly sublime Chinamans Beach.

Crescent Head

MACLEAY VALLEY COAST

IN THE WAVE-SOAKED MINDS of many surfers, Crescent Head on the New South Wales mid-north coast isn't a town but a perfectly peeling right-hand point break, and for good reason. It's one of the longest and most consistent waves in Australia, where 300m (984ft) rides in the company of leaping dolphins aren't unusual. Being roughly halfway between Sydney and Byron Bay has also made it an obligatory stop on any north-coast 'surfari', ever since *Surfing World* founder Bob Evans brought Midget Farrelly and a few other longboarding talents to test the waters back in 1963. Crescent Head became one of Australia's first National Surfing Reserves, in 2008, in recognition of its importance to Australian surfing culture. There's also a quiver of beautiful surf beaches south of Crescent, along the mostly sealed Plomer Rd – such as Racecourse, Delicate Nobby, Limeburners Creek, Big Hill and Point Plomer – all with back-to-nature campgrounds.

At Crescent itself, a short amble uphill from the beachfront carpark – permanently lined with vans and surfers of all ages waxing up – brings you to Little Nobby headland. Enjoy spectacular views: surfers dotting the takeoff zone, long peeling waves wrapping around the north side of the headland, Australia's only six-hole golf course (which has ocean views from every green) and the long, patrolled beach (accessible by a ramp in front of the surf club) stretching north to the distant blur of Hat Head.

GETTING THERE

Crescent Head is 428km (266 miles) or a half-day drive north of Sydney/Warrane. There's also a 34km (21-mile) coastal walk and 4WD-only road from Port Macquarie, south of Crescent. It's a seven-hour train trip from Sydney to Kempsey; in school holidays there are buses from Kempsey to Crescent Head (25 minutes).

You don't even have to surf to immerse yourself in Crescent's surf scene. Just drop into the Green Room (surf slang for 'tube') cafe for a smoothie, browse vintage surfwear store Cheetah Five (a nose-riding move in longboarding) or check into the Sea Sea Hotel that opened in late 2024. Its hip millennial vibe, beach-chic retro styling and Sydney room rates might be a long way from the days when visiting surfers could survive on $10 a day, but Crescent has certainly evolved since then – without forgetting its roots as the kind of place a beach-lover of any age can happily return to, year after year, knowing all the important elements will always be there.

Palm Beach

SYDNEY/WARRANE

THE MOST NORTHERLY of Sydney/Warrane's northern beaches, Palm Beach has always had an air of mystery, despite standing in for the fictional Summer Bay in the long-running television drama *Home & Away.* It's an apt stage name, for 'Palmie' is all about carefree, sun-drenched days, uncrowded surfs and languid summer nights, thanks to its day-trip distance from busier parts of the city. This sweep of sand stretches 2.3km (1.5 miles) from the hammerhead Barrenjoey Headland (and Barrenjoey Lighthouse, at its northern end) to Palm Beach's more bourgeois southern corner, with its genteel waves, celebrity residents and members-only beach clubs. There are also two surf-lifesaving clubs, founded in 1921 and 1946, that patrol the long beach on weekends and public holidays.

The half-hour trek to the lighthouse is worth it for the panoramic views. Look north past the sphinxlike Lion Island and across the mouth of the Hawkesbury River to the New South Wales Central Coast, and south along the isthmus that separates Pittwater, a sailor's paradise, from Palm Beach's wilder ocean side.

GETTING THERE

Palm Beach is 43km (27 miles) north of Sydney Harbour. Travelling by bus from the city takes about two hours. There's also a seaplane service from Rose Bay, on demand.

The Pass

BYRON BAY

FOR TENS OF THOUSANDS OF YEARS, the Arakwal people of the Bundjalung Nation have gathered on the beaches of Cape Byron/Walgun to fish, feast and share stories. Today, surfers gather in droves at one of its best-known beaches, The Pass, to ride one of the world's longest right-hand point breaks, as swimmers bob in its azure waters (patrolled during peak summer and Easter holiday periods). Yet the rich Aboriginal history of The Pass remains everywhere, from the region's largest midden (a pile of shell and bones) found beside the boat ramp, to the culturally significant native wildlife – from koalas to brush turkeys – that can be spotted in the subtropical rainforest fringing its shores.

Even if you're not a beach person, an Aboriginal walking tour with Arakwal Bundjalung woman Delta Kay from Explore Byron Bay, who hosts several Cape Byron/Walgun tours, is a must-do. Learn the significance of this coastal idyll as you walk in the footsteps of Delta's ancestors. And don't forget to look up for Miwing, the white-bellied sea eagle, an important totem animal for Arakwal people that can often be spotted circling overhead.

On the foreshore of The Pass you'll also find barbecue facilities and the wheelchair-accessible Palm Valley Currenbah walking track, which makes a 700m (0.5-mile) loop through a lush palm rainforest. You can also follow the Cape Byron walking track from here to Australia's most easterly point; allow at least an hour to complete the 3.7km (2.5-mile) loop, which also takes in Wategos Beach – home to some of Australia's most exclusive real estate – and peaceful Little Wategos, accessible only on foot.

A rocky outcrop rises from the northern end of The Pass, with stairs leading up to a platform offering impressive vistas from the Cape Byron Lighthouse to the east, around to the distinctive and culturally significant peak of Wollumbin (formerly Mt Warning) to the northwest. Below, rock pools provide hours of fun for the young and young at heart.

Sunset is a magical time at The Pass, with a tangerine glow cast across the water as surfers chase the last waves of the day. Breathe deep and take it all in.

GETTING THERE

With limited parking at the beach, the scenic 20-minute walk along the sand from central Byron (or the wheelchair-accessible foreshore pathway), is the best way to get to The Pass. There's also limited paid parking at neighbouring Captain Cook and Clarkes beaches.

Wattamolla Beach

ROYAL NATIONAL PARK, SYDNEY/WARRANE

ON THE SOUTHERN EDGE of New South Wales' capital lies Australia's oldest national park, gazetted in 1879, and still one of the country's favourites – partly for its magnificent Royal Coast Track, a 26km (16-mile) hike that follows the park's coastal curves; and partly for a small, perfectly formed beach about halfway along its coastal edge. But Wattamolla is more than just a beach. Just 400m (1312ft) from the car park, a 6m (19.7ft) waterfall pours itself into a clear lagoon framed by sandstone cliffs and a soft-sand

beach. Walk across that beach and you can plunge into an ocean inlet that resembles a large, open-ended saltwater pool, indented from the rocky coastline. While the beach and its surrounds are unpatrolled, Wattamolla's lagoon is often family friendly, depending on the tides and creek levels. There's also a grassy picnic area, popular with day-trippers and hikers on the Royal Coast Track, where it's not uncommon to see wallabies and echidnas (there are no kangaroos or koalas in this park).

GETTING THERE

Wattamolla Beach is 48km (30 miles) south of Sydney/Warrane, the last 11km (7 miles) a scenic drive through Royal National Park. The car park gets busy on summer weekends, so arrive early or visit on a weekday.

Cabarita Beach

TWEED REGION

SET BETWEEN THE TOURIST MAGNETS of the Gold Coast to the north and Byron Bay to the south, the laid-back Tweed region receives far fewer visitors to its clutch of long, sandy beaches fringed by pandanus trees. For swimming, surfing, accessibility and coastal scenery, it's hard to beat Cabarita Beach's namesake beach. The swell wraps around the rocky point of Norries Head to create a fine right-hander at 'Caba', with the headland also providing protection from southerly winds. Tucked inside the headland, the beach's southern end is known as Norries Cove, while the main northern end of the beach is patrolled by volunteer lifesavers from the Cabarita Beach Surf Life Saving Club, where beach wheelchairs are available.

Toilets, covered barbecues and picnic tables are located in Lions Park at the foot of Norries Head. Follow the short walking trail around the headland for great whale-watching opportunities in winter or to check the conditions at Maggie's Beach to the south.

GETTING THERE

Cabarita Beach is 30km (18.5 miles) south of Gold Coast Airport, or about an hour by bus from Tweed Heads on the New South Wales–Queensland border.

Emily Bay

NORFOLK ISLAND

AT FIRST, THIS SMALL AUSTRALIAN ISLAND looks like a chunk of New Zealand's bucolic North Island that has broken off and drifted 1100km (683 miles) north. But despite being only 8km (5 miles) long and 5km (3 miles) wide, Norfolk Island is vividly, defiantly, more than just a Mini-Me of its two largest neighbours. For one thing, its history reads like an epic adventure tale: from the seafaring Polynesian settlers who called the island home from 1200 to 1600; to two brutal convict eras, during which Norfolk became known as the 'Hell in the Pacific'; to the arrival, in 1856, of 194 Pitcairn Islanders descended from HMS Bounty mutineers and their Tahitian families, whose culture and language still infuse daily life on Norfolk.

Ringed by high volcanic sea cliffs and surrounded by deep ocean trenches and undersea mountains, Norfolk Island is also ruggedly natural. There's a national park, multiple walking trails, and a botanical garden. The eponymous pine trees grow everywhere; even the main settlement is called Burnt Pine. And because of strict biosecurity regulations, most of Norfolk's food is grown, caught, foraged or made on the island, even coffee and wine.

Christian's GLAAS BOHTAM BOET
"Mavatua"

It all comes together at Emily Bay. One of the island's best swimming beaches – and picnic spots – just happens to be within the Kingston UNESCO World Heritage Site, surrounded by Norfolk Marine Park. It's a stone's throw from the ruins of the island's notorious penal settlement, and includes a pier, boathouses, prisoners' barracks and a cemetery overlooking the sea. You can swim in water that's as clear as a glacial stream but warm all year round, because Norfolk lies at the same latitude as Byron Bay in Northern New South Wales. The sandy beach isn't patrolled, but low headlands partially enclose the bay, keeping its waters calm and family friendly. Swim out a little way and you can even snorkel over a coral reef, though the snorkelling is arguably better at neighbouring Slaughter Bay (which is more inviting than its name). A turquoise lagoon fringed by coral, its temperate and tropical fish like wrasse and parrotfish are known to swim right up to your mask.

GETTING THERE

Norfolk Island is 1400km (870 miles) east of Byron Bay. Flights to the island depart from Brisbane/Meanjin, Sydney/Warrane and Auckland. Emily Bay is 5 to 10 minutes' drive from the main township of Burnt Pine (be mindful of the island's cows, which have right of way).

Reef Beach

SYDNEY HARBOUR NATIONAL PARK, SYDNEY/WARRANE

AT FIRST, IT DOESN'T SEEM POSSIBLE: a small, north-facing slip of sand surrounded by bushland right at the entrance to Sydney Harbour, gateway to one of Australia's largest cities, and just across the water from Manly. But Reef Beach, in Sydney Harbour National Park, is a natural time capsule, a glimpse of what this coastline might have looked like in 1788, when British colonists first encountered, in this very bay, the people of the Eora nation. More recently, this was a clothes-optional beach for

a couple of decades, starting in 1976. When the popular coastal walking track, the Manly Scenic Walkway, opened in 1988, it wasn't unusual for bushwalkers passing by to count naked sun-worshippers among the local fauna. Today Reef Beach is a much-loved refuge for locals and families seeking serenity and a calm place to swim, where tall, salmon-barked angophora trees lean graciously over slabs of sandstone at the southern end of the beach, creating shady oases perfect for picnics on summer days.

GETTING THERE

Reef Beach can only be reached on foot or by boat (or kayak or stand-up paddleboard). It's a 50-minute harbourside stroll from Manly along the Manly Scenic Walkway, the spectacular 10km (6-mile) track between Manly and Mosman's Spit Bridge.

Number One Beach

SEAL ROCKS

THE FIRST BEACH YOU SEE on your left as you drive into the hamlet of Seal Rocks, Number One is a north-facing beauty with a gentle right-hand point break at its eastern end, and calm waters ideal for families. The caravan park is just across the road, there are picnic tables and an accessibility ramp. Up and over the hill, past Seal Rocks' only shop, lies Boat Beach, where tractors launch small fishing boats straight off the sand. It's ideal for both swimming and snorkelling; the three-hump rock island just off the beach is a sanctuary for grey nurse sharks. And just south of Seal Rocks, a gravel road leads to three more beaches popular with experienced surfers: Lighthouse (Sugarloaf Point Lighthouse stands at its northern end), Treachery (synonymous with its sprawling family-owned campground behind the dunes) and Submarine Beach (named after a 1945 Dutch submarine-wreck), also called Yagon after the national park campground located at its northern end.

GETTING THERE

Seal Rocks is a tiny town encircled by Myall Lakes National Park, 239km (148.5 miles) north of Sydney/Warrane. The nearest train station is in Taree, on the Sydney–Brisbane XPT line. From Taree, it's about 90 minutes by car to Seal Rocks.

Pambula River Mouth Beach

PAMBULA

THE COASTLINE BECOMES more wild and rugged as you travel down the New South Wales South Coast. Just 50km (31 miles) from the Victorian border as the crow flies, Pambula's trio of beaches offer a well-rounded taste of the region's coastal beauty. There's the main Pambula Beach, a wide, patrolled surf beach (with beach wheelchairs available) sweeping north to Merimbula. Just around its southern headland is Lions Park/Jiguma Beach, a small dog-friendly cove fringed by coastal bushland. But arguably the finest patch of sand is found around the corner again at the mouth of the Pambula River, where the idyllic turquoise waters of the river flow into the sapphire sea. Protected from northerly and easterly winds, it's the kind of beach where you could spend all day counting the shades of blue created by the shifting sands beneath the shallow water. Stretch your legs on the 1km (0.6-mile) return Pambula River walking track beginning at the southern end of the beach, or bring a kayak or stand-up paddleboard and embark on a scenic paddle upriver.

Like most river-mouths, it can be dangerous swimming here during an outgoing tide.

GETTING THERE

Pambula is 460km (286 miles) or a six-hour drive south of Sydney.

Balmoral Beach

SYDNEY/WARRANE

WITH MORE THAN 100 BEACHES to choose from in Sydney/Warrane, the city's excellent harbour beaches are often overlooked. Captured in the works of some of Australia's most prolific painters – from Arthur Streeton to Ken Done – unpatrolled Balmoral Beach is a special place for many Sydneysiders, and its calm waters popular with families.

Separated from Edwards Beach by the tiny Rocky Point Island, the 840m (2638ft) arc of Balmoral Beach lies on the traditional lands of the Cammeraygal people of Sydney's North Shore, who

have camped, hunted and feasted along this caramel sandstone coastline for generations. A tramline from the city opened in 1922, improving access to Balmoral's enclosed bathing area built in 1899. A grand bathing pavilion, a rotunda for brass-band concerts and a wide promenade was added in the 1930s. While the tram is long gone, the Balmoral Baths and the Art-Deco rotunda and pavilion (now a celebrated restaurant) remain, adding an air of regality fitting for a beach named for Queen Victoria's Scottish castle.

GETTING THERE

Buses from the city (Wynyard) take approximately 20 minutes to reach the junction of Spit Rd and Awaba St. From here it's a steep 600m (1968ft) downhill walk to the beach. There's limited beach-front parking.

Honeymoon Bay

**JERVIS BAY,
SHOALHAVEN**

FAMOUS FOR ITS BLINDING WHITE SANDS, azure water and abundant marine life, including dolphins, fur seals and wintertime whales, Jervis Bay has long been a popular beach destination on the New South Wales South Coast. Scooped out of the Beecroft Peninsula on the bay's northern headland, tiny Honeymoon Bay is a suitably romantic spot for a refreshing dip.

Culturally significant to the Jerrinja people, who believe revered ancestor Bundoola resides at its tip, the Beecroft Peninsula has been used for Australian Defence Force training activities since the 1800s. For this reason, Honeymoon Bay, along with the peninsula's handful of other beaches and walking tracks, are only open on weekends, public holidays and school holidays. Surrounded by native bushland, the small, shallow cove of Honeymoon Bay is nearly enclosed by its sandstone headlands. It is particularly popular with campers, but you can visit for the day to swim, snorkel, paddle, clamber around the rocks or laze on its blond sands.

GETTING THERE

Honeymoon Bay is a 45-minute drive from Huskisson in central Jervis Bay, or a three-hour drive from Sydney/Warrane. Check the Department of Defence's 'Beecroft Weapons Range and Peninsula' Facebook page for access updates – the area is closed when the car park reaches capacity.

North Smoky Beach

HAT HEAD NATIONAL PARK, MID-NORTH COAST

SPIED FROM ABOVE, set beside Smoky Cape Lighthouse on the Mid North Coast of New South Wales, North Smoky Beach is a pirate's treasure, made all the more precious by the fact that it can only be reached on foot. Native casuarina and pandanus trees provide natural shade for your beach picnic, and that teal water is impossible to resist. Just remember to swim, surf or bodysurf with care: there are no lifeguards within cooee of North Smoky. At low tide, cross the sand spit to a large dreamy rock pool on a small

islet; or wander around the rocks to another nameless, but just as perfect, beach. Or, just offshore, watch sea eagles gliding over the grassy hump of Green Island, a popular boat-dive site. Back up at the lighthouse, the highest in New South Wales, hang out with grazing eastern grey kangaroos, look south to the dazzling never-ending-ness of South Smoky Beach, and watch for pods of migrating humpback whales (May–November).

GETTING THERE

To get to North Smoky Beach follow the 0.8km (0.5-mile) Jack Perkins Walking Track downhill from Smoky Cape Lighthouse, 8km (5 miles) from the township of South West Rocks, which is 461km (286 miles) north from Sydney/Warrane.

Ned's Beach

LORD HOWE ISLAND

SIR DAVID ATTENBOROUGH once described Lord Howe Island as "so extraordinary it is almost unbelievable". It might be only 11km (7 miles) long and just over 2km (1.2 miles) wide, but this little nature-centric island – World Heritage–listed way back in 1982, its waters protected by a marine park – punches above its weight in terms of conservation and biodiversity. And on the northeast coast of this natural wonderland lies Ned's Beach.

Wade into the gin-clear water to swim or snorkel (borrow equipment from an honesty box beside the picnic tables) and you'll immediately find yourself knee-deep in fish – mullet, garfish, silver drummer, spangled emperor, kingfish – all utterly unafraid of you. They usually stick to the shoreline, so if you gently push through the mob, you'll soon leave them behind and be drifting over Ned's coral reefs; psychedelic in colour and activity, thanks to ocean currents that allow tropical, subtropical and temperate species to coexist here. You might even see a few turtles or a (harmless) Galapagos shark.

GETTING THERE

Lord Howe Island is a two-hour flight from Sydney/Warrane, Newcastle/Muloobinba, Port Macquarie or the Gold Coast. Rental bicycles are the best way to get around when you're there. Ned's Beach is a five-minute bike ride from town and from Lagoon Beach.

Although it's unpatrolled, Ned's cove-like shape makes it generally safe for swimming, and there are surf-able waves on the edges of the reefs in the right conditions. (Blinky Beach, at the other end of the island, is the place to surf beach breaks.) Other adventure options include sea kayaking (with a guide) to the Admiralty Islands just offshore, and diving, as these volcanic islands have more than 25 world-class dive sites with corals, large schools of fish and visibility up to 40m.

Lord Howe is also a hot spot for seabirds. Hundreds of thousands breed on the island every year, including red-tailed tropicbirds, which you can see from Ned's between November and June when they wheel overhead, their red tails trailing like ribbons as they come and go from their nests in the neighbouring Malabar cliffs. Then there are the shearwaters, also called muttonbirds. At dusk between September and May, the well-kept lawn behind Ned's Beach is the stage for a nightly spectacle: hundreds of muttonbirds gliding to shore after a day at sea and crash-landing at your feet before waddling into the dense palm forest in search of their burrows.

Victoria

LEFT Mount Martha Beach
ABOVE Squeaky Beach

Bells Beach

SURF COAST

ONE OF AUSTRALIA'S MOST LEGENDARY surfing beaches, Bells was enshrined in pop culture when Patrick Swayze's adrenaline-junkie character, Bodhi, waits his whole life to surf its fabled '50-year swell' in the 1991 action film *Point Break*.

But before its movie stardom, Bells Beach came from humble beginnings. Originally inaccessible, motorbikes and bulldozers eventually cleared a path to the beach in the 1950s, and in 1962 it hosted its first ever surfing contest when a gaggle of local surfers gathered at the frigid water's edge.

Fast forward over 60 years and Bells enjoys a global reputation as one of Australia's – and the world's – best surfing beaches. The humble community-run Easter Rally has morphed into the Rip Curl Pro, the longest-running event in competitive surfing and an iconic stop on the World Surf League Championship Tour.

Crowds flock to the dramatic red-clay cliffs framing this natural amphitheatre every year over the April Easter weekend, watching as surfers carve, duck-dive and glide along enormous 6m (20ft) waves. The thigh-burning surf forms when Southern Ocean waves wrap around the point and hit an exposed reef, creating a surging wall of water with a right-hand break perfect for carving with a surfboard.

GETTING THERE

Located on Victoria's Great Ocean Road, Bells Beach is 5km (3 miles) from the closest town of Jan Juc, or a 90-minute drive southwest of Melbourne. You can also get here by bus. Stairs lead down from the car park to the small beach.

The winner earns the coveted Rip Curl Pro trophy and the glory of ringing its famous silver bell. Etched into the gold plate are the names of past winners, including Mick Fanning, Kelly Slater, Stephanie Gilmore and Gail Cooper, who took out the title a whopping 10 times in the 1960s and '70s.

With its challenging waves, ever-changing conditions and lack of surf lifeguards, Bells Beach isn't the place for a casual dip. Instead, you can enjoy the spectacular vantage points from the clifftop car park, overlooking the water where surfers practice their skills year-round, especially in the early morning.

Eager surfers can practise their skills at nearby Torquay or Anglesea, while swimmers should head to Cosy Corner in Torquay, which has a patrolled beach with sheltered conditions. Elsewhere, you can dive into the region's rich surfing past at the Australian National Surfing Museum in Torquay.

Childers Cove

GREAT OCEAN ROAD

LIKE A POT OF GOLD waiting at the end of a rainbow, Childers Cove is a secluded spot just before the end of Victoria's famed Great Ocean Road driving route. From the small carpark at the top of the escarpment, steep wooden steps descend to a narrow crescent of sand bookended by hulking cliffs that thrust towards Bass Strait.

When the tide is out, you can poke around in the rock pools, but swimmers should be wary. A combination of a shallow beach, which drops off suddenly at the cove's entrance, and the encircling cliffs mean the cove is home to a near-constant rip. There are no facilities onsite and the beach is not patrolled.

Childers Cove was the scene of one of Victoria's most tragic wrecks when the ship *Children* lost direction in hurricane-force storms and smashed into the cliffs. Salvaged items, including an anchor, cannon and bricks, can be seen at Flagstaff Hill Maritime Museum and Village in Warnambool.

GETTING THERE

Childers Cove is in Nirranda, about 25 minutes east of Warrnambool by car. As you drive along Childers Cove Road, you'll also pass Sandy Cove, where you can see a trio of limestone stacks just offshore.

Squeaky Beach

WILSONS PROMONTORY NATIONAL PARK, WEST GIPPSLAND

ENCLOSED BY IMPRESSIVE GRANITE boulders at either end, Squeaky Beach is a standout in Wilsons Promontory National Park, a rugged slice of wilderness at the southernmost tip of mainland Australia, bordered by Victoria's largest marine national park. The fine, rounded grains of quartz sand on this snow-white beach compress underfoot, creating a high-pitched squeak – hence the name. Wander between the huge boulders at the northern end of the beach and splash in hidden rock pools, or dive into the bay's crystalline waters; at their most inviting during

the warmer months (particularly November to March). Connecting Squeaky Beach with Picnic Bay and Whisky Bay to the north, the 6.2km (3.9-mile) Three Bays Walk is another way to immerse in this spectacular stretch of coastline. Allow two hours each way.

There's camping just around the headland at Tidal River; perfectly placed to savour a Squeaky Beach sunset. Native wildlife-watching opportunities also increase during the golden hour – look for wombats, kangaroos, emus and other critters.

GETTING THERE

Squeaky Beach is 222km (138 miles) or about a three-hour drive from Melbourne/Narrm. Park behind the beach or walk here from Picnic Bay or Tidal River. Alternatively, catch a Yarram-bound bus to Fish Creek, and take a taxi from there.

Mount Martha Beach

MORNINGTON PENINSULA

IF YOU'RE FLYING into Melbourne/Narrm, you'll likely see Mount Martha Beach before you leave the airport, thanks to its brightly painted beach huts splashed across billboards welcoming you to Victoria.

Nearly 100 weatherboard huts were first built in the mid-19th century and, despite not having running water or electricity and some falling into disrepair, they're much-loved local landmarks; privately owned and usually locked.

Lapped by the calm waters of Port Phillip Bay, the beach itself runs for 2km (1.2 miles), split down the middle by a shallow creek. At the northern end lies Mount Martha Life Saving Club, which patrols the beach from November to May, and a yacht club teaching kids and adults how to handle a jib. Wheelchair-friendly beach matting extends from the Life Saving Club down to the waterline, and the club has an accessible changeroom with showers.

Just across the road is a handy village of fish-and-chip shops, supermarkets and delis; perfect for picking up supplies for a sunset picnic by the water.

GETTING THERE

Located on the traditional lands of the Bunurong people, Mount Martha Beach is an easy one-hour drive from Melbourne along the coast. Arrive early to score a coveted parking spot.

Wreck Beach

GREAT OTWAY NATIONAL PARK, GREAT OCEAN ROAD

DESCENDING THE 366 STEEP STEPS from the cliffs down to Wreck Beach is a gamble. At high tide you'll find just a short belt of sand and heaving surf, with nowhere to go but back the way you came. But time your visit for low tide and you'll discover an abundance of history in the rock pools.

In the mid-19th century, decades before concrete was first poured on Victoria's Great Ocean Road, this infamous stretch of shallows and hidden reefs was feared among sailors, who dubbed it the Shipwreck Coast.

An estimated 660 ships met their fate along the coast, many of them drawn to Melbourne/Narrm during Victoria's gold rush from 1851 to 1896, in hopes of cashing in on the city's immense wealth. Today, stories of ruin and survival are scattered like flotsam from Anglesea to Port Fairy, including the remains of two shipwrecks at Wreck Beach.

The steep staircase leads you down to 2km (1.2 miles) of beach backed by a natural amphitheatre of wind-buffered golden cliffs. There are no facilities, and the rough surf makes the water unsuitable for swimming, but wander about 400m (1312ft) from the bottom of the stairs and you'll find a pair of anchors with fascinating stories.

GETTING THERE

Wreck Beach is a three-hour drive from Melbourne/Narrm along the Great Ocean Road. From the car park, a short bush trail leads to a staircase to the beach.

Jutting out of a figure eight–shaped rock pool are the rusted remnants of *Marie Gabrielle's* anchor, with other parts scattered in the pools surrounding it. While carrying tea from China to Melbourne in 1869, *Marie Gabrielle* was blown off course by a heavy gale and crashed into Moonlight Head. Everyone onboard survived but the tea could not be saved.

The *Fiji* wasn't as lucky. After leaving Hamburg, the ship was tragically close to the end of its journey when bad weather and faulty navigational equipment caused it to crash into Moonlight Head in 1891. Locals sent lifesaving gear from Port Campbell, which included a vital length of rope that went missing when they arrived at the wreck.

The *Fiji's* rusted anchor is all that remains on the beach, but climb the steps at the northern end to see a white tombstone dedicated to the lost crew, including a poignant mention of the cook, 'name unknown', who perished with them.

Sorrento Back Beach

MORNINGTON PENINSULA

FOUND ALONG THE 'BACK BEACH' of coastal town Sorrento, this ocean-swimming spot is a sickle-shaped stretch of golden sand tucked into the underbelly of the Mornington Peninsula. It's popular with surfers and fishers year-round. During summer, the sand sizzles and squeaks, and the shallow rock pools are a treat for soaking your toes and searching for critters, including crabs, anemones and Victoria's emblematic weedy sea dragon.

A handful of walking trails start from the beach, including

a short circuit up the hill to a historic lookout rotunda, a 1.5km (1-mile) walk to Sorrento's main shopping strip, and a scenic 3km (2-mile) walk along Coppins Track to nearby Diamond Bay.

A large car park and kiosk overlook the water (both can get very busy in summer), and the beach can be accessed using stairs or a wheelchair-friendly ramp. Sorrento's Surf Life Saving Club patrols during busy times of the year, mainly from December to April, and visitors should check the latest surf report.

GETTING THERE

From Melbourne/Narrm it's a 90-minute drive south along the Mornington Peninsula to Sorrento. Allow extra time on weekends and during school holidays, as roads become congested with Melburnians flocking to this popular beach haven.

Ninety Mile Beach

EAST GIPPSLAND

FROM THE TOP of Ninety Mile Beach's dunes, you can look both ways and see nothing but unending sand. Free from rocky outcrops to obstruct the view, Australia's longest single beach is an unbroken stretch of dunes, shallow inlets and lagoons that separates Gippsland Lakes from Bass Strait.

Festooned along its length are the sleepy coastal towns of Woodside Beach, Seaspray, Golden Beach and – the largest and most popular – Lakes Entrance. In summer the area is popular for fishing in the surf, beachside camping and long walks, while in winter you can try your hand at spotting humpback and southern right whales migrating up the coast.

To really connect with nature, pitch a tent or drive your caravan to one of 20 free camping spots behind the sand dunes. Most sites have toilets and paid showers, and most importantly, unrivalled access to the water.

Beaches are patrolled during summer at Woodside, Seaspray and Lakes Entrance, with beach wheelchairs and accessible toilets available at Lakes Entrance Main Beach and Seaspray Surf Life Saving Club.

GETTING THERE

Ninety Mile Beach is a three-hour drive east of Melbourne/Narrm, cutting a trail inland through the regional towns of Warragul, Morwell and Traralgon before arriving at Lakes Entrance.

Smiths Beach

PHILLIP ISLAND/MILLOWL

ON AN ISLAND crowded with good beach spots, Smiths Beach is small but mighty. Bookended by bushy headlands, the 1km (0.6-mile) golden bar of sand enjoys consistent waves thanks to its southwestern position, making it a treat for surfers, body-boarders and paddleboarders.

At low tide, the compacted sand is ideal for beach cricket or rugby, while snorkellers will find anemones, sea urchins, starfish and more in fizzing rock pools at both ends of the beach.

Phillip Island's most famous residents, the adorable fairy penguins, prefer to stay close to their burrows on Summerland Beach. While away the day at Smiths, grab fish and chips from Cowes or San Remo, then drive across the island in time for Summerland's nightly Penguin Parade at sunset.

Smiths Beach has a ramp leading from the sealed car park down to the beach. The car park has toilets (including an accessible toilet), changerooms and outdoor showers. Lifeguards patrol from late November to late February. Nearby Island Surfboards & Surf School offer surfboard hire and surfing lessons.

GETTING THERE

Known as Millowl to its Bunurong Traditional Custodians, Phillip Island is 140km (87 miles) or a two-hour drive east of Melbourne/Narrm and accessed by a bridge from mainland San Remo.

Thurra Beach

CROAJINGOLONG NATIONAL PARK, EAST GIPPSLAND

BEGINNING AT THE MOUTH of the Thurra River and stretching west to Hicks Point, Thurra Beach is as dramatic as it is wild, especially when waves crash into the granite headlands and fill the air with salty spray.

It's found on the isolated coastline of Croajingolong National Park, named for the Indigenous Krauatungalung people. Swim or paddle your kayak in the tannin-tinted lagoon, hike along a short track beneath coastal woodlands to discover the calf-burning Thurra River Dunes or enjoy some laid-back beach fishing.

Rips are frequent, so most visitors stick to swimming in the

river-mouth and close to the beach's sandbars. The beach isn't patrolled by lifeguards and sometimes the road can be blocked after storms. Check the latest weather and road reports on the Parks Victoria website.

Stay in the historic lighthouse keeper's cottage at Hicks Point, which has guided tours of the lighthouse precinct, or there's the popular Thurra River Campground, located right at the river's mouth. The campgrounds have shared picnic tables, fireplaces with barbecue plates and non-flush toilets. Bookings are essential.

GETTING THERE

Thurra Beach is a seven-hour drive east of Melbourne/Narrm, passing through the large regional towns of Warragul, Traralgon and Lakes Entrance, where you can collect camping supplies.

Blanket Bay

GREAT OTWAY NATIONAL PARK,
GREAT OCEAN ROAD

EVEN MORE SCENIC than Victoria's Great Ocean Road is the Great Ocean Walk, a 110km (68.4-mile) hiking route hugging the wild and dramatic coastline between Apollo Bay and the Twelve Apostles. For many hikers, Blanket Bay is a favourite stop.

Framed by the forested hills of Great Otway National Park, Blanket Bay is a small blond beach with an intertidal reef that makes its shallow waters safter for swimming than many other beaches on this treacherous coast (p131), but always take care. It also has rock pools to investigate, and views along the rugged coastline to lap up. But you don't need to hike in to enjoy this spot, as there's an access road and a day-use area next to the beach.

Blanket Bay's basic campground also ranks among the best on the Great Ocean Walk, popular for its protected location, proximity to the beach and pretty setting fringed by ferns. Rise early to bask in the glow of sunrise at this east-facing slice of coastal wilderness before your next day on the trail – or morning on the beach.

GETTING THERE

Blanket Bay is 232km (144 miles) or a 3.5-hour drive from Melbourne/Narrm. The final 6km (3.5 miles) is a 2WD-accessible dirt road.

Eastern Beach Reserve

GEELONG/DJILANG

RIGHT ON THE BAY-FACING DOORSTEP of Melbourne's little sister Geelong/Djilang, Eastern Beach Reserve has a carnival atmosphere throughout summer. The star attraction is the semicircular sea bath enclosed by a promenade, where swimmers can walk out to a floating diving tower, paddle to pontoons, or practise their breaststroke in the ocean lap pool.

Originally built in the 1930s, Victoria's only surviving ocean pool has retained its old-world charm thanks to its preserved Art-Deco features, which include the promenade, two red-brick pavilions containing changerooms and kiosks, and a shallow children's pool crowned with a bubbling fountain. Close to the water is a shaded playground and terraced lawns overseen by the city's famous bollards, which are colourfully painted to resemble lifeguards.

Real lifeguards patrol the reserve during the summer months. Accessible rubber matting runs from the car park to the water's edge, and beach wheelchairs are available to hire free of charge.

In 2024, Eastern Beach Reserve's unique history and architecture saw it join Victoria's Great Bathing Trail – an 885km (550-mile) route connecting the best bathing spots across the state.

GETTING THERE

Geelong is a 70-minute drive west of Melbourne along the M1 freeway.

Tasmania

ABOVE Wineglass Bay
RIGHT Binalong Bay

Wineglass Bay

FREYCINET NATIONAL PARK, FREYCINET PENINSULA

IT'S ONE OF THE MOST PHOTOGRAPHED sights in Australia: an arc of silica-white sand curving around a bay shading from bright turquoise shallows to indigo where it meets the Tasman Sea, the entire scene encircled by the dusky pink Hazards Range and the forested hills of Freycinet National Park. But that means you probably won't be the only person photographing it; the lookout atop Mt Amos, a steep 2.5km (1.5-mile) climb from the nearest car park, is one of the most popular spots in Tasmania.

For a little headspace, and to put yourself in the picture, take a 30-minute bush stroll from the lookout down to the beach itself, keeping your eyes peeled for echidnas and Bennetts wallabies. When you get there, be sure to walk barefoot on that 1.5km (1-mile) arc of fine sand and swim in the (chilly) water. Two circuit tracks in Freycinet National Park, one 11km (7 miles) and the other 27km (17 miles), promise an even more immersive experience; both include a beach-walk along Wineglass Bay and a night amid blue gums and Oyster Bay pines at the small, free campground at the beach's southern end. A less strenuous and more accessible Wineglass-viewing option is the 500m (1640ft) boardwalk at Cape Tourville, a 7km (4.3-mile) drive east of Coles Bay, the main settlement on the peninsula.

It's a little-known fact that Wineglass Bay isn't just named for its shape. Between the 1820s and the 1840s, whalers in small boats harpooned southern right whales migrating up the east coast then towed them to this beach to butcher them, turning the bay blood red, like wine. When right whale numbers dwindled, the whalers moved offshore to hunt sperm whales, until the entire industry collapsed in the 1880s. In 1916, the Freycinet Peninsula was declared a national park, the first in Tasmania/Lutruwita, and whale populations began to recover. Today, Great Oyster Bay, just across the isthmus from Wineglass Bay and visible from Mt Amos lookout, is one of the best places in Australia to see southern-right whales, between May and November.

GETTING THERE

Coles Bay is 192km (119 miles) north-east of Hobart/Nipaluna and 173km (107.5 miles) south-east of Launceston. Buses travel to Coles Bay from Hobart and St Helens, 114km (71 miles) up the coast. There are several campgrounds in the Freycinet area, but book ahead; sites for mid-December to early February are usually allocated by ballot in August.

Fortescue Bay Beach

TASMAN NATIONAL PARK,
TASMAN PENINSULA

WEAVING ALONG THE TOWERING SEA CLIFFS of the Tasman Peninsula, the four-day Three Capes Track features views from the wonderfully wild southeastern tip of Tasmania/Lutruwita. Among the trail's many highlights is the idyllic beach at the finishing point, where it's customary for weary walkers to strip off for a restorative dip in its azure waters, which can be chilly even at the height of summer. But you don't need to do the multiday hike to swim here.

Framed by wooded slopes rising up to 200m (656ft) high, the 700m (0.5-mile) Fortescue Bay Beach on the eastern side of the peninsula is sheltered from the pounding Southern Ocean surf, making the unpatrolled sweep of powder-white sand ideal for less confident swimmers, supervised children and paddlers. Two national park campgrounds behind the beach (Banksia and Mill Creek) offer opportunities to enjoy this remote slice of Tasmania for longer. If you're feeling energetic, it's a 9.5km (6-mile) return hike from the southern end of the beach to the dramatic Cape Hauy. Keep an eye out for Tasmanian short-beaked echidnas en route.

GETTING THERE

Located on the traditional lands of the Oyster Bay Nation, Fortescue Bay is 90km (56 miles) or a 90-minute drive from Hobart/Nipaluna.

Binalong Bay

BAY OF FIRES/LARAPUNA

THE LONG MAIN BEACH in front of the small town of Binalong Bay in the northeast corner of Tasmania/Lutruwita is part outdoor gallery, part artwork, with nature the artist. The sand is as white as a canvas. The sky's blue is dialled up to eleven. The rounded granite boulders are cloaked in tangerine, a creeping lichen resembling splashed paint; and lapped by an aquamarine sea, clear as Champagne, that glints in the sunshine. All of it tempting you to strip off, dash across the soft sand and plunge in. But beware – swimming in such a scene can be life-changing, like a saltwater ice-bath on steroids, even in February, the warmest month in Tasmania. On a more prosaic level: some sections of this unpatrolled beach, and others in the Bay of Fires area, can have steep drop-offs, so swim with care and with a friend.

GETTING THERE

Binalong Bay is 11km (7 miles) northeast of St Helens and 175km (109 miles) east of Launceston, at the southern end of the Bay of Fires Conservation Area that stretches 50km (31 miles) up the coast to Eddystone Point. Beachside camping is available at neighbouring Swimcart Beach on the road to The Gardens.

Hopground Beach

MARIA ISLAND/WUKALUWIKIWAYNA

PROTECTED IN ITS ENTIRETY by Maria Island National Park, 115.5 sq km (44.5 sq mile) Maria Island/ Wukaluwikiwayna has a number of beautiful beaches. Given there's a hulking quartet of concrete silos rising up from the northern end of Darlington Bay, not everyone would immediately pick Hopground Beach as the island's best. But its prime position, surrounded by history and wildlife, gives it an edge.

For generations, the Puthikwilayti people of the Oyster Bay Nation lived in harmony with the natural rhythms of this ancient volcanic island, with evidence of shellfish feasts still found on many of its beaches. A less subtle relic of the island's history is the Darlington Probation Station, a convict settlement founded in

1825. Plagued by escapes, it was closed just seven years later, with the remaining convicts shipped down to Port Arthur.

Now a World Heritage–listed convict site, the settlement's 14 intact buildings and ruins are just a short walk from the beach, where ferries arrive from the mainland. However, the silos are the legacy of Italian entrepreneur Diego Bernacchi, who secured a long-term lease of the island in 1884, planted a vineyard on the sloping hillside above Darlington Bay, and set up a cement works to use the island's limestone deposits. Bernacchi's island business empire eventually went belly-up, with the silos – along with the home he built in 1890, now used by the Maria Island Walk – left standing as reminders of his ambitious pursuits.

GETTING THERE

Maria Island/Wukaluwikiwayna is a 45-minute ferry ride from Triabunna, which is 86km (53.5 miles) or a 75-minute drive northeast of Hobart/Nipaluna.

Now uninhabited except for a few park rangers, Maria Island has become famous for its wildlife, a legacy of the 1960s importation of several mainland species considered to be under threat, such as Cape Barren geese, forester kangaroos and Flinders Island wombats, followed by a group of Tasmanian devils in 2012. Nowhere are the island's now-famed wombats more abundant than the grassy foreshore of Hopground Beach, especially at dawn and dusk. This grassy area doubles as the island's campground, so you can pitch up just steps from the sand and wake to wombats (and equally cute pademelons) grazing alongside your tent.

Whether you're just visiting for the day or camping for a night or two, the clear, cool waters of Hopground Beach invite an invigorating dip, or at least a contemplative stroll along its white sands.

Disappointment Bay

KING ISLAND

THIS REMOTE BEAUTY OF A BEACH owes its name to a tragic shipwreck, one of more than 140 that haunt the coastline of King Island. At dawn on 13 May 1835, the ship *Neva,* transporting female convicts, free settlers and their children from Ireland to Sydney, struck submerged rocks. Of the 239 passengers, 224 lost their lives. It was one of the worst shipwrecks in Australia's history. Today Disappointment Bay is a 1.7km (1-mile) stretch of white sand and smooth rocks bookended by Cape Wickham and its 1861 lighthouse to the west, and the headland of Rocky Point to the east. A favourite with surfers, along with the nearby Martha Lavinia Beach, it's best on westerly swells that refract off the cape. It's also a world-class picnic spot, the perfect place to enjoy some award-winning cheeses from King Island Dairy – perhaps a Cape Wickham Double Brie or a Roaring Forties Blue – while gazing out at the Southern Ocean.

GETTING THERE

King Island is in Bass Strait, about 80km (50 miles) off the northwestern tip of Tasmania/Lutruwita. There are regular commercial flights to the island from Melbourne/Narrm, Launceston and Burnie. Disappointment Bay is at the island's northern end, 43km (27 miles) from Currie, the main town.

Trousers Point Beach

FLINDERS ISLAND

MORE THAN 100 BEACHES have been scalloped out of the rugged coastline of Flinders Island, the largest island in the Furneaux Group off the northeast coast of Tasmania/Lutruwita. Fringed by tangerine lichen–covered boulders, they're all beautiful, and never crowded. But there's something extra special about 'Trousers', sheltered from the prevailing westerly wind and backdropped by the hulking granite peak of Mt Strzelecki. The shallow waters surrounding Flinders Island mean the water is warmer than you might expect at this latitude, and there's good snorkelling around the picturesque headland – look out for weedy seadragons. On the foreshore you'll find toilets, a campground, and the trailhead for the 2km (1.2-mile) return Trousers Point coastal walk, one of Tasmania's 60 Great Short Walks.

GETTING THERE

Trousers Point Beach is 18.5km (11.5 miles) south of Whitemark, the island's main town. A weekly car ferry runs between the island and mainland Bridport and takes about eight hours. Charter flights from Bridport take about 30 minutes.

The Neck

BRUNY ISLAND

THE NECK IS AN ENIGMA wrapped in a beach towel. Halfway down the hourglass-shaped Bruny Island, this sandy isthmus connects North and South Bruny (once two islands), and separates the D'Entrecasteaux Channel from the wild Tasman Sea. To get your bearings, deep-breathe the cleanest air in the world and pay your respects to Truganini, the Neunonne warrior who died in 1876 (she and her people were the Traditional Custodians of Bruny), climb the 300m (984.3ft) staircase to Truganini Lookout halfway along The Neck, for windy, widescreen views. Back at sea level, boardwalks lead to a viewing platform on the dunes where, just after dark between September and February, clusters of little penguins amble ashore to their nests, while thousands of shear-waters fall out of the sky and scurry to their own burrows. By day, The Neck is beachcombing heaven but swimming isn't recom-mended; dangerous rips are common and the beach is unpatrolled (try Adventure Bay in South Bruny instead).

GETTING THERE

Bruny Island is 20 minutes by car ferry from Kettering, 37km (23 miles) south of Hobart/Nipaluna. From the wharf it's a 24km drive (15 miles) to The Neck. There's a national park camp-ground at the southern end of the isthmus.

Boat Harbour Beach

BOAT HARBOUR BEACH

THE SERENE LOVELINESS of Boat Harbour Beach belies its location on the north coast of Tasmania/Lutruwita, facing Bass Strait, the strip of wild water between the island state and mainland Australia famous for its ship-wrecking storms. But this squeaky-sand cove embraced by green hills, with low headlands protecting its aqua-blue waters, is one of Tasmania's best-kept secrets, a timeless seaside hamlet with beachfront cottages, no shops or traffic lights and a permanent population of about 80. It's also supremely family friendly. There's a playground, picnic tables and public barbecues, grassy areas for beach cricket or a game of Frisbee, and coastal walking trails in nearby Rocky Cape National Park. The beach is patrolled on weekends and public holidays between December and March, when the water is as warm as it gets. The Boat Harbour Beach Surf Life Saving Club also has the only cafe/restaurant in the village, right on the beach, where you can enjoy a flat white with your fish and chips while contemplating another swim.

GETTING THERE

Boat Harbour Beach is on Tasmania's north coast, 80km (50 miles) west of Devonport, where the *Spirit of Tasmania* car ferries arrive from Geelong/Djilang in Victoria, and 176km (109.5 miles) northwest of Launceston.

South Cape Bay

SOUTHWEST NATIONAL PARK

LYING AT THE SOUTHEASTERN TIP of Southwest National Park, at the eastern end of the 85km (52.8-mile) South Coast Track, one of Australia's most challenging multiday hikes, South Cape Bay offers a taste of Tasmanian wilderness usually reserved for experienced hikers. Getting there involves a two-hour bushwalk from a dead-end road in the former whaling settlement of Cockle Creek, the most southerly township in Australia. And when the track emerges at an exposed ledge and stairs descending to the sand, prepare to be amazed. Even on calm days, Southern Ocean swells direct from Antarctica thunder onto this remote seaweed-strewn beach, rumbling its cobblestones and reshaping its sandy shoreline. In stormy weather, icy Roaring Forties gales threaten to blow you off your feet. Naturally, swimming isn't recommended; the sea is cold and unpredictable, mobile reception is limited and rescue unlikely if you get into trouble. Better to have a dip back at Cockle Creek, in the tranquil waters of Recherche Bay.

GETTING THERE

South Cape Bay is a 16km (10-mile) return hike from Cockle Creek, which is 120km (74.5 miles) from Hobart/Nipaluna and the furthest south you can drive in Australia. There's a free campground at Cockle Creek, no bookings required.

Landing Beach

MACQUARIE ISLAND

THERE IS NO SQUEAKY WHITE SAND. The water is hypothermically cold. It's likely to be raining or blowing a gale. But Landing Beach is one of Australia's best for other reasons, like the sheer magnificence of its Southern Ocean location, its mountains – the island is an uplifted undersea mountain range – and the astounding abundance of wildlife that envelops you as soon as you step ashore. This World Heritage–listed wildlife sanctuary is home to countless fur seals; as many as four million

penguins – kings, royals, gentoos and rockhoppers; and up to 90,000 elephant seals, great boulders of flesh that roar at each other on the beach itself. Then there are its estimated 3.5 million seabirds, including skuas and giant petrels that accompany you like feathered drones as you wander the island's rocky paths. It's no wonder Antarctic explorer Sir Douglas Mawson described this wild little island as 'one of the wonder spots of the world'.

GETTING THERE

Macquarie Island is 1500km (932 miles) southeast of Hobart/Nipaluna. The only way to get there as a tourist is to join a small-ship expedition cruise run by operators such as Aurora Expeditions or Heritage Expeditions, departing from Hobart, or Dunedin in New Zealand.

South Australia

ABOVE Vivionne Bay
LEFT Greenly Beach

Seal Bay

KANGAROO ISLAND

ALMOST A THIRD OF KANGAROO ISLAND (KI) is protected by national parks and reserves, preserving its wilderness and the wildlife that depends on it. Fire has long shaped this terrain, but the catastrophic 2019–2020 bushfires redrew the landscape, tearing through nearly half of the island. Scorched but not silenced, KI rallied – saplings took root, nature rebounded, and the community set to work strengthening fragile ecosystems against future fires.

Spared from the flames, Seal Bay Conservation Park, 57.5km (36 miles) southwest of Kingscote, provides a precious glimpse into the lives of one of the planet's most vulnerable marine mammals. Despite its name, this isn't the domain of true seals, but rather the endangered Australian sea lion, the country's only endemic pinniped. Endearingly dubbed 'puppies of the sea,' these lively lumps have hung out here for generations, making this one of the last places to witness them romping through their natural habitat.

GETTING THERE

Seal Bay is 88km (55 miles) from KI's Penneshaw car-ferry terminal. The crossing to Cape Jervis takes 45 minutes, followed by a 106km (66-mile) drive to Adelaide/Tarntanya. Or catch a 45-minute flight from Adelaide to KI and hire a car or join a tour.

Dotted along the shore, sea lions lounge on ivory sands, tumble through the surf and galumph their way up the beach. The experience is both immersive and informative, with ranger-led tours providing a rare, up-close encounter, unpacking the sea lions' cheeky behaviour and fragile existence.

The research tour is more in-depth, granting exclusive insights into the tracking and monitoring efforts that help protect these imperilled creatures. With fewer than 12,000 sea lions left in the wild – 85% residing along South Australia's coastline – Seal Bay is at the heart of conservation efforts. To ensure their protection, the beach is strictly off-limits unless accompanied by a guide.

For an elevated perspective, the park's 900m (2953ft) wheelchair-accessible, self-guided boardwalk tour rises steadily above the fore-dunes, threading a string of lookouts peering down on the colony and the Southern Ocean into the distance.

If watching sea lions basking by the water's edge has you craving a beach break, neighbouring Bales Beach, just 1km (0.5 miles) off Seal Bay Rd, delivers an uncrowded stretch of soft white sand, ideal for a post-tour decompress and a refreshing dip. The safest area to swim is by the rock pool directly in front of the car park.

Salmon Hole

BEACHPORT

A 600M (1968.5FT) CRESCENT of soft, blond sand curls beneath sculpted fore-dunes, cradling a lagoon so luminous it seems to hold the sky. Salmon Hole is a contradiction in motion – the Southern Ocean's bluster is tamed by a belt of weathered beach rock, forming a sheltered, sapphire sanctuary.

A rare family-friendly refuge along the Limestone Coast's wild shoreline, its waters remain calm while swells crash beyond the reef. Near the beach's southern entrance, tidal pools brim with tiny marine life, inviting young explorers to search for underwater mysteries. At the northern end, Post Office Rock (Point William) juts seaward – a weatherworn spit tethered to a rocky tombolo, offering precarious yet rewarding sunset views.

As the beach's name suggests, Australian salmon thrive here. Cast a line at high tide during twilight hours for a chance at landing a 4kg (8.8lb) catch. Just north, Beachport Conservation Park spills into the dunes, its bird-filled wetlands, walking trails and shaded campgrounds a natural extension to this secluded cove.

GETTING THERE

One of the star attractions along the Bowman Scenic Dr, Salmon Hole sits alongside the small coastal town of Beachport, 381km (237 miles) southeast of Adelaide/Tarntanya via the Princes Hwy.

Stokes Bay

KANGAROO ISLAND

HIDDEN ALONG KANGAROO ISLAND'S north coast, Stokes Bay is guarded from the outside world by an amphitheatre of bluffs and a fortress of boulders. Entry requires a short but sure-footed adventure through shadowy crevices.

From the Stokes Bay car park, follow the signs along a winding path that slices into the headland. Duck through low-hanging bedrock, step over jagged ledges, and let the sound of crashing waves guide you through the narrow cracks. Then, just as the trail tightens, the limestone walls part to reveal a dazzling 500m (1640ft) of powdery white sand and aquamarine waters stretching ahead. At low tide, a natural rock pool forms at the western end, offering a protected spot to wade and snorkel among starfish and darting crabs.

Beyond Stokes Bay, Kangaroo Island's north coast is studded with enticing dips – Emu Bay, Snelling Beach, and the lesser-known Western River Cove. If you'd rather linger, Stokes Bay Campground offers a basic but wildlife-rich overnight stay, steps from the sand.

GETTING THERE

Kangaroo Island is 45 minutes by plane from Adelaide/Tarntanya or about four hours by car, including the ferry from Cape Jervis. Stokes Bay is 38km (23.5 miles) from the island's airport, and 90km (56 miles) from its Penneshaw ferry terminal.

Seacliff Beach

ADELAIDE/TARNTANYA

ADELAIDE/TARNTANYA'S LAID-BACK BEACHES are often overlooked in favour of the region's famed festivals, food and wine. Perched on the city's southern fringe, Seacliff/Wita-wattingga captures the capital's seaside serenity, its 1km (0.6-mile) beach blissfully removed from the urban buzz.

The clear, sheltered waters draw morning swimmers. Beneath the surface, Seacliff's resident stingrays, unbothered by human company, glide gracefully through the shallows; paddleboarding offers a bird's-eye view of these gentle creatures, with rentals available from the Brighton & Seacliff Sailing Club. Next door, the Surf Life Saving Club hires beach wheelchairs, rolling out an access mat to the water's edge on weekends and public holidays.

A historic pub, two chilled cafes and a waterfront caravan park make it easy to settle in, but the coastline tempts further exploration. A breezy 20-minute stroll along the esplanade leads north to Brighton jetty, while the scrub-lined 5km (3-mile) Marion Coastal Trail climbs south. For a cultural detour, a cliffside track ascends to the Tjilbruke Monument lookout above the beach, honouring the Kaurna Dreaming Story of the freshwater spring below.

GETTING THERE

Seacliff Beach is 16.8km (10.4 miles) from Adelaide's city centre by car or a 25-minute train ride on the Seaford line to Seacliff Railway Station.

Almonta Beach

COFFIN BAY NATIONAL PARK

ANCHORED TO THE TIP of the Eyre Peninsula's windswept prow, Coffin Bay National Park sprawls across 300 sq km (120 sq miles) of wild coastal frontier. Beneath the tsunamic dunes and jagged limestone, Almonta Beach unspools its vast ribbon of pearlescent sands toward the horizon.

A 30-minute drive from oyster-famed Coffin Bay, on the traditional lands of the Nauo people, who fished and foraged these waters for millennia, Almonta has long been shaped by nature's forces. The sand here sings underfoot, fine enough to squeak with your steps. Kangaroos lounge in the scrub, while white-bellied sea eagles carve the updrafts, eyes locked on the turquoise shallows. Though the currents can be fierce, the beach's fringes hold gentler adventures – rock pools alive with starfish, swirling shells and other marine curiosities exposed at low tide.

Beyond the beach, six remote 4WD-only campgrounds dot the park's rugged interior, each unpowered and wonderfully secluded. For those without an off-road rig, Yangie Bay Campground provides a base among sheltered inlets, where kayaking and bushwalking trails weave through the wild.

GETTING THERE

Almonta Beach is 706km (438.5 miles) or an eight-hour drive from Adelaide/Tarntanya. Golden Island Beach car park has the easiest access; avoid Almonta's eastern entrance unless you're driving a 4WD.

Vivonne Bay

KANGAROO ISLAND

STRUNG ALONG KANGAROO ISLAND'S wild southern rim, Vivonne Bay is a striking contrast of wild and serene – an unhurried 6km (3.5-mile) arc of bone-white sand lapped by the swirling blues of the Southern Ocean. Backed by scrub-topped dunes and a sleepy village, this slice of solitude still feels like a secret.

Its waters, among the island's clearest, shift from glassy calm to churning swells, their intensity softened by Point Ellen's protective headland. The safest swim spot is south near the jetty, where the bay's sheltered nook keeps waves at bay. Further north, the Harriet River mouth feeds into the sea, creating ever-shifting sandbanks where dangerous currents lurk. For surfers, the bay's clean right-handers fire up on bigger swells, though you'll need to bring your own board – rentals are nonexistent.

A short drive unlocks Little Sahara's sandboarding dunes, the eerie limestone labyrinth of Kelly Hill Conservation Park, and Flinders Chase National Park's legendary rock formations – all within half an hour's drive.

GETTING THERE

Kangaroo Island can be reached from Adelaide/Tarntanya by plane (45 minutes) or car (about four hours, including the ferry from Cape Jervis). Vivonne Bay is 47km (29 miles) from the island's airport and 90km (56 miles) from the Penneshaw ferry terminal.

Long Beach

ROBE

A SVELTE ARC OF SILKEN SAND tracing the edge of Guichen Bay, Long Beach is Robe's 12km (7.5-mile) coastal show-piece – an open, drive-on strip where turquoise surf froths against a pale-gold shore. One of South Australia's few vehicle-friendly beaches, it's a magnet for 4WD-ers, who roll in with Eskies (portable cooling containers for food/drinks) and fishing rods.

Surfers chase moderate peaks along the bay, with the best breaks near the third ramp, off Steven Woolston Rd. Backed by low dunes tufted with coastal heath and sea rocket, the shore is prime territory for birdlife – watch for hooded plovers skittering between tidelines and oystercatchers probing the foam.

The safest swim zone is at the beach's southern entrance, in front of the foreshore reserve, where calm waters stay splash-friendly and rip-free. For better accessibility, head to small Town Beach in nearby Robe, just in front of the visitor centre, where free beach wheelchair hire ensures a smooth roll across the sand and into the shallows.

GETTING THERE

Long Beach, just north of historic Robe on the Limestone Coast, lies 334km (207.5 miles) southeast of Adelaide/Tarntanya. Access via 4WD is permitted from the second ramp – best tackled at low tide.

Greenly Beach

COULTA, EYRE PENINSULA

LASHED BY THE Southern Ocean's squall, Greenly Beach is a wilder kind of paradise tucked along the Eyre Peninsula's west coast beach crawl. A refuge for solitude-starved surfers, its waves peel off a central reef, offering the first consistent swell north of Coffin Bay.

Back on shore, soft sand and salt-washed pools make for cool plunges and envy-inducing photos. Flanking the dunes, sandstone bluffs crumble to the sea, carving calm recesses for patient anglers to await nibbles from Australian salmon, trout, mullet and the odd

Tommy Ruff (Australian herring). Greenly Rock Pool, at the beach's northern edge, is a natural saltwater spa, refreshed twice daily by the turquoise tide. Just south, no-frills campsites overlook the beach, delivering front-row seats to raw coastal sunrises.

For a panoramic perspective, Mt Greenly/Millapa looms 250m (820ft) above the heathland. A steep but rewarding two-hour return hike delivers a god's-eye view over Nauo Country, sweeping across the Great Australian Bight and inland toward the vast Lake Greenly/Puwanna.

GETTING THERE

Greenly Beach is 638km (396.5 miles) west of Adelaide/Tarntanya, the journey looping around the St Vincent and Spencer Gulfs via the Lincoln Hwy. The nearest town, Coffin Bay, is 42.5km (26 miles) south of the beach – around a 35-minute drive.

Port Willunga Beach

ADELAIDE/TARNTANYA

ROLLING OFF MCLAREN VALE'S vine-woven hills, Port Willunga – Wirruwarrungga or Ruwarunga to its Traditional Kaurna Custodians – is a coastal relic of a bygone era. The sun-bleached remnants of a long-forgotten jetty rise solemnly from the shallows, while honeyed limestone cliffs shelter cavernous alcoves once used by fishers to stow their boats. Offshore, the wreck of the *Star of Greece,* a three-masted iron barque claimed by the sea in 1888, lies draped in kelp, luring snorkellers and divers into its eerie depths.

Shielded from brisk southerlies, the beach is an open invitation for lazy swims, while the clifftops frame panoramic views along the Fleurieu Peninsula's rugged headlands. A short climb inland leads to the Star of Greece restaurant, where just-caught seafood meets a stellar regional wine list. Sunset here is pure theatre – the sky flares in molten hues, jetty ruins casting long, skeletal shadows across the shore. For those chasing quiet, midweek mornings often leave the sands untouched, save for the footprints of shorebirds tracing the tide.

GETTING THERE

Port Willunga Beach is 47km (29 miles) south of central Adelaide/Tarntanya. Driving is the fastest option, but public transport – a train to Seaford and a short bus ride – gets you there in around 1.5 hours.

Dolphin Beach

DHILBA GUURANDA-INNES NATIONAL PARK, YORKE PENINSULA

HEMMED IN BY WIND-SCOURED CLIFFS and rolling dunes, Dolphin Beach is a secluded pocket of wilderness within Dhilba Guuranda-Innes National Park at the tip of Yorke Peninsula. Named for the resident bottlenose dolphins that surf its waves, this remote cove is a living postcard of the wild. Ospreys hover on coastal updrafts and tammar wallabies peek from the scrub. At first light, fresh kangaroo tracks tattoo the sand, while hooded plovers flit along the water's edge, a tiny yet tenacious reminder of enduring wildlife.

Fringing the beach, hardy coastal heath flourishes, with saltbush and wildflowers igniting the dunes after winter rains. Rock pools shimmer along the headlands, teeming with anemones and crabs, while snorkellers drift through shoals of glistening baitfish.

Overnighting here means camping in the dunes or booking a restored heritage house in the nearby gypsum-mining ghost town of Inneston. As dusk settles, prepare for one of South Australia's most theatrical seascapes – crashing waves, salt-laced air, and an endless sprawl of stars.

GETTING THERE

Dolphin Beach is located on the traditional lands of the Narungga people, 284km (176.5 miles) west of Adelaide/Tarntanya, near the town of Marion Bay.

Ocean Beach

COORONG NATIONAL PARK

AN ENDLESS RIBBON of wind-carved sand stretches 194km (120.5 miles) from the mouth of the Murray River to Cape Jaffa, south of Adelaide/Tarntanya, standing as a natural barrier between Coorong National Park's wetlands and the restless Southern Ocean. Australia's longest dune system remains largely untouched – claimed only by seagulls and the adventurous few who arrive by 4WD, boat or an achingly long walk.

Beyond the dunes, the Coorong's marshy wilds flutter with life, an internationally significant bird sanctuary where some 230 species nest across salt-crusted pans and ephemeral soaks. This slice of Ngarrindjeri Country rewards photographers and bird-watchers. Pelicans wheel overhead, congregating in this vast, watery nursery, while ducks, swans, cormorants, terns and grebes dabble in the shallows. A vital pit-stop on the East Asian-Australasian Flyway, the Coorong shelters migratory visitors such as the critically endangered eastern curlew.

For intrepid campers, Ocean Beach delivers solitude in its rawest form – windswept, beachfront and unreachable without a 4WD. These no-frills, no-crowd campsites hunker between the dunes, promising an infinite sky, with only rumbling waves breaking the silence.

GETTING THERE

Coorong National Park's easiest 4WD ocean access is via 42 Mile Crossing, 3km (2 miles) off the Princes Hwy, with a wheelchair-accessible toilet and shady picnic area.

Stony Point Beach

WHYALLA

WITH ITS ROCKY SHORELINE limiting beach activities and the neighbouring Port Bonython hydrocarbon-processing facility detracting from its natural beauty, Stony Point might not scream 'best beach'. But if you time your visit right, a life-changing snorkelling experience awaits.

Each May, tens of thousands of giant cuttlefish converge in this area of the Upper Spencer Gulf Marine Park to literally mate themselves to death, with all but a few disintegrating by the end of August, before the next generation has hatched. The cunning

games and dramatic colour displays exhibited by males to lure a mate for breeding are mesmerising to watch, and with all the action going on at shallow depths, you barely need to dive below the surface.

Guided snorkelling and diving tours operate from the industrial town Whyalla, or bring your own gear. With the water temperature averaging a chilly 13°C (55.5°F) during the peak spawning months, a 5–7mm (0.2–0.3in) wetsuit with a hood, and booties, are recommended. There is a shelter, picnic tables and changerooms at Stony Point, and a campground at nearby Point Lowly.

GETTING THERE

Stony Point is 34km (21 miles) northeast of Whyalla, or 400km (248.5 miles) north of Adelaide/Tarntanya.

Western Australia

ABOVE Hellfire Bay
RIGHT Cossies Beach

Elephant Rocks

WILLIAM BAY NATIONAL PARK, DENMARK REGION

IN A HIDDEN COVE on the south coast of Western Australia lies one of the state's most striking coastal landscapes. Colossal boulders rise from the shallows, like a herd of bathing elephants, slowly meandering out to sea. Dating back over 1.5 billion years, this geological marvel was once a vast mountain range – smoothed by time and tide into the rounded granite domes seen today.

Perched on the edge of William Bay National Park, Elephant Rocks holds deep significance for the Menang people, who have cared for this land for thousands of years. Today, its crystal-clear shallows and otherworldly geology create a breathtaking backdrop for swimming, picnicking and photography.

The beach is unpatrolled. Visitors should take care on slippery rock surfaces and be aware of the occasional strong current surging through the bay. The adjacent Greens Pool, an eight-minute walk away, is a similarly picturesque boulder-fringed bay for swimming, snorkelling and sunbathing, with a little more space to spread out on the shore.

GETTING THERE

Elephant Rocks is 15km (9 miles) west of Denmark in William Bay National Park. A short trail leads from the car park to the beach. Parking is limited in peak season; plan to arrive early.

Lucky Bay

CAPE LE GRAND NATIONAL PARK

IMAGINE SAND SO WHITE and so fine it whistles underfoot, and water in shades of blue so beautiful it doesn't seem real. Cradle it between scenic granite outcrops linked by bushwalking trails and add a few kangaroos, and you have Lucky Bay.

Stretching for 20km (12.5 miles), this protected bay near Esperance/Kepa Kurl in the state's southwest is right up there with Australia's dreamiest. Float in the crystalline water, cast a line at a secluded fishing spot, or gaze out to the ocean between July and

October for the chance to see migrating whales. From November to early March, consistently windy days make the shallow bay popular with kitesurfers.

Come just for the day or camp under a moonlit sky at the western end of the beach, keeping in mind that the 56 spots in this national park campground can book out in advance. Tame kangaroos are commonly sighted on and around the beach at dawn and dusk; admire them from a distance.

GETTING THERE

Lucky Bay is 64km (40 miles) or a 50-minute drive east of Esperance, which is another 700km (435-mile) drive (or a short flight) from Perth/Boorloo. There is no public transport to Lucky Bay.

The Basin

ROTTNEST ISLAND/WADJEMUP

MANY AUSTRALIAN BEACHES have human-made ocean pools, but Rottnest Island/Wadjemup has The Basin – a natural pool of turquoise water so clear and calm it feels like slipping into a cool salty bath. A three-minute cycle (or 10-minute walk) from Thomson Bay, the island's main township, and even closer to its campground, this elliptical lagoon carved into the limestone reef is one of the island's most beloved natural swimming pools.

If you've yet to understand the enduring appeal of 'Rotto', spend a warm summer's day at The Basin and you'll soon see why Western Australian locals return year after year. By midmorning, the ding of bike bells fills the air as families arrive – bicycles being the main form of transport on the carless island – with kids all smiles after spying sleepy quokkas, the island's beloved pint-sized marsupials, en route. Beach towels unfurl on the soft white sand, and candy-coloured snorkels bob in the shallows.

The Basin's north-facing position protects it from strong swells, providing ideal conditions for snorkelling and leisurely swims (though keep an eye on kids at this unpatrolled spot). Its variety of limestone ledges and channels are suitable for beginners and experienced snorkellers, with its reef home to a swirling symphony of marine life, from blue-barred parrotfish to western buffalo bream and the striped stingaree, a small species of stingray.

GETTING THERE

Multiple daily ferries connect Rottnest Island with Fremantle/Walyalup (25 minutes), Perth/Boorloo (90 minutes), and Hillarys (45 minutes).

Peckish? There's a Mediterranean restaurant right on the shoreline; and Pinky's Beach Club, just a five-minute stroll away, is a great spot for relaxed coastal dining. You'll also find newly refurbished outdoor showers, BBQs and toilet facilities at The Basin.

Long before it was a tourist playground, Wadjemup or 'the place across the water where the spirits are', was an important ceremonial site for Whadjuk Noongar people, evidenced by the ancient tools and weapons found on its shores. After colonisation, Rottnest became the site of one of Australia's most notorious Aboriginal prisons, with hundreds of men and boys forcibly taken from their homelands across Western Australia and incarcerated here. At least 373 of them died here. Today, Wadjemup remains a place of remembrance, and efforts continue to acknowledge this chapter of the island's history. Thompson Bay's Rottnest Museum is an excellent spot to learn more about its complex history on your way to The Basin.

Roebuck Bay

BROOME/RUBIBI

THE COLOURS OF the Western Australian outback are dialled up to maximum saturation at Roebuck Bay, where the red pindan soil of the Kimberley melts into the milky cyan waters of the Indian Ocean southeast of Broome/Rubibi. It's hard to believe that the golden sands of Cable Beach (p238) are just a 30-minute drive away when you arrive at the most photogenic stretch of Roebuck Bay's beach, just south of the Broome Bird Observatory, where offshore mangroves make for surreal drone photography, particularly at high tide. As the tide ebbs, it reveals a rippling carpet of mudflats where the local Yawuru people have fished, hunted and gathered seafood for millennia.

One of Australia's 67 Ramsar wetland sites, Roebuck Bay teems with birdlife; make sure you look out for the brolga, far eastern curlew, black-necked stork and the eastern yellow wagtail among the many other species. With saltwater crocodiles on patrol here rather than lifeguards, swimming is not recommended.

To admire a similar beach aesthetic closer to Broome, make your way to Simpsons Beach, which curls northward from the Broome Port Jetty.

GETTING THERE

Broome is a 2.5 hour flight from Perth. The Broome Bird Observatory is 28km (17.5 miles) from central Broome via a 2WD-accessible dirt road.

Meelup Beach

DUNSBOROUGH

COASTAL PEPPERMINT and eucalypt trees perfume the salty air at Meelup Beach, a north-facing bay where the ocean typically rests in perfect stillness, more like a lake than the open sea. Tucked in the gentle curve of Geographe Bay, Meelup Beach is a place of shifting blues – pale aquamarine in the shallows, deepening to sapphire as the seabed falls away.

For thousands of years, the Wardandi people of the Noongar Nation have gathered here, drawn to the abundance of fish and the moon's silvery path over the bay. The name Meelup means 'place of the rising moon', and when conditions are right, a luminous reflection stretches across the water, an ancient spectacle still celebrated today.

While unpatrolled, Meelup's calm waters are ideal for families and ocean swimmers, and long summer days spent idling between sand and sea. It's also popular with stand-up paddleboarders and snorkellers, and there's a wheelchair-accessible pathway from the car park all the way to the water's edge.

GETTING THERE

Meelup Beach is 4.5km (3 miles) east of Dunsborough in Meelup Regional Park. Accessible by car, bike or the scenic Meelup Trail, it has parking that fills quickly in peak season (from December to February); arrive early or explore nearby beaches if it's full.

Cossies Beach

DIRECTION ISLAND, COCOS (KEELING) ISLANDS

CLOSER TO INDONESIA than Western Australia, the twin set of tropical atolls known as the Cocos (Keeling) Islands offer a Southeast Asian island escape with no passport required. Just two of its 27 islands – West Island and Home Island – are inhabited; the remainder primed for tropical-island escapism.

A day-tripper favourite, Direction Island cradles a generous lick of ivory sand gently sloping into gin-clear water. With toilet facil- ities, wood-fired barbecues, walking trails and shaded shelters on

the foreshore, Cossies Beach is an undeniably idyllic location for a leisurely day of beach picnicking. But the highlight for confident swimmers is snorkelling The Rip, a channel at the southern end of the beach where the current whisks you past vivid corals, turtles, rays, reef sharks and tropical fish galore. Swim fins are a safety essential for snorkelling The Rip; for a more relaxed experience, book a local skipper to pick you up after you've floated along.

GETTING THERE

Flights from Perth to the Cocos Islands take just under five hours, with a stop in Christmas Island. Public ferries run from West Island and Home Island to Direction Island (and back) on Thursdays and Saturdays.

Hamelin Bay

MARGARET RIVER REGION

ON A STILL DAY, Hamelin Bay feels almost otherworldly – a long sweep of white sand where the Indian Ocean fades into the sky. But it's not just the scenery that makes this place special. The bay is home to several species of stingray, some spanning up to 2m (6.5ft), their broad, velvety wings often seen gliding through the shallows.

Hamelin Bay was once a timber port, and its submerged shipwrecks hint at its past, now forming artificial reefs teeming with herring, skippy (silver trevally), and octopus, drawing experienced

divers when conditions allow. The bay's calm waters are ideal for snorkelling, stand-up paddleboarding and kayaking, while beyond the headland, more exposed swells appeal to keen surfers.

Situated on the traditional lands of the Wardandi people, Hamelin Bay is a family favourite for its sheltered waters, with the adjacent Hamelin Bay Holiday Park offering the chance to stay right by the shore. As tame as the stingrays may seem, they should always be observed from a safe distance at the unpatrolled beach.

GETTING THERE

Hamelin Bay is 30km (18.5 miles) north of Augusta and 15km (9 miles) south of Margaret River. It's best reached by car, with parking near the beach.

Wharton Beach

CAPE LE GRAND NATIONAL PARK

AT WHARTON BEACH, the world looks like it's been dialled up to full saturation. From the iridescent aquamarine swell, to the blindingly white sand and the lush green backdrop of Cape Le Grand National Park – it's a landscape as vivid as a fever dream.

Located on the traditional lands of the Wudjari people, Wharton Beach is best known for its vast, uncrowded expanse of sand, and the playful pods of dolphins often seen surfing the beach breaks. A favourite among local longboarders and bodysurfers, Wharton Beach offers some of the most consistent waves in the Esperance region. It's also one of the few beaches in the area where 4WDs are allowed on the sand, making it easy to find a private patch of paradise.

Despite its remoteness, Wharton Beach is popular in summer, when calm conditions and warmer sea temperatures draw swimmers and snorkellers in droves. Unpatrolled and untouched by development, Wharton Beach is pure, wild beauty – Esperance at its absolute best.

GETTING THERE

Wharton Beach is 80km (50 miles) east of Esperance, which is 700km (435 miles) or a 95-minute flight from Perth/Boorloo.

Turquoise Bay

NINGALOO/NYINGGULU COAST

THIS ARID STRETCH OF COASTLINE in Cape Range National Park on Western Australia's Coral Coast is among the most ecologically rich in the country. Just metres from shore, the World Heritage-listed Ningaloo Reef – one of the world's longest fringing reefs – unfolds beneath the surface.

Slip into the shallows, and the famous drift snorkel at Turquoise Bay carries you effortlessly above a kaleidoscope of marine life. Parrotfish nibble coral, blue-spotted stingrays skim the sandy floor, and if you're lucky, you might spot a reef shark on patrol. From March to August, Ningaloo welcomes awe-inspiring whale sharks, while humpback whales migrate along the coast later in the year.

Ningaloo Reef supports over 500 species of fish, 300 coral species, and marine megafauna including dugongs and manta rays. The accessible reef allows snorkellers to experience an underwater world usually found in the open ocean. However, it is under threat from coral bleaching, pollution and human activity. Conservation efforts and sustainable tourism play a crucial role in protecting its future.

For thousands of years, the Baiyungu, Thalanyji and Yinigurdira peoples have maintained a deep connection with the Ningaloo area – evidenced in the ancient fish traps, middens and ceremonial sites found along the coast. Following the 2023 signing of an historic Indigenous Land Use Agreement, Traditional Custodians now jointly manage this special place with the State Government, with Indigenous-led tours offering deeper insights into Ningaloo's heritage.

There are no lifeguards or facilities (beyond an accessible toilet), and the occasional strong currents require caution. May to November is the best time to visit, with the chance to see whale sharks. Stay in nearby Exmouth or camp by the beach in national park campgrounds.

GETTING THERE

Turquoise Bay is 63km (39 miles) southwest of Exmouth and is accessible by car. It takes just under two hours to fly to Exmouth from Perth/Boorloo, or about 13 hours to drive. To access the drift snorkel, park at the Drift Loop parking area and walk south along the beach for about 200 metres before entering the water. Exit before reaching the sandbar forming the western arc of the bay.

Misery Beach

ALBANY/KINJARLING

LAPPED BY THE GLASSY WATERS of King George Sound, this secluded ribbon of powdery white sand on the traditional lands of the Menang people feels like a hidden paradise. It wasn't always this way, having been named for the stinking whale remains dumped here by a nearby whaling station that operated until 1978. Today, the only splashes of red come from the crimson-streaked sky above the tranquil bay at dusk.

Misery Beach's allure is no longer a secret: in 2022 it was named by the national tourism board as Australia's best beach. Protected from the Southern Ocean's wild swells, the 200m (656ft) bay offers calm waters for swimming and snorkelling. The surrounding granite outcrops create natural windbreaks, making it an ideal spot to linger with a picnic or take in the stillness. Be on the lookout for its resident seals, dolphins and migratory whales. The neighbouring Isthmus Hill, once a whaler's lookout, offers breathtaking views across the coastline.

GETTING THERE

Misery Beach is 22km (14 miles) or a 30-minute drive south of Albany in Torndirrup National Park. There's a small car park, with a short walk to the beach. There are no public transport services.

Hellfire Bay

CAPE LE GRAND NATIONAL PARK

ITS NAME MAY SUGGEST something hellish, but this stretch of the Western Australia's south coast is pure serenity – a crescent of impossibly soft, white sand meeting the electric blue of the Southern Ocean. Situated in the Cape Le Grand National Park, Hellfire Bay is cradled by granite headlands and sculpted dunes, making it one of the more protected bays along this sun-drenched coastline on the traditional lands of the Wudjari people of the Noongar Nation.

Though not patrolled by lifeguards, the calm, translucent waters of Hellfire Bay make it a family favourite, with shady patches of sand found beneath its granite boulders. There are barbecue facilities and picnic tables for seaside feasting and, if you can drag yourself away from the sand, the 800m (0.5-mile) trail at the eastern end of the beach leads to the more secluded but similarly sublime Little Hellfire Bay. The more challenging Coastal Trail weaves past both beaches on its 20km (12.5-mile) route.

GETTING THERE

Hellfire Bay is 56km (35 miles) east of Esperance, about a 45-minute drive via Cape Le Grand Rd. With no local public transport services, you'll need your own wheels to reach this destination.

Cape Leveque/ Kooljaman

DAMPIER PENINSULA

CLASPING THE NORTHERNMOST TIP of the remote Dampier Peninsula, Cape Leveque is a place of striking contrasts, where mighty pindan cliffs rise from bone-white sand, their rugged edges softening as they crumble toward the Indian Ocean.

This is Bardi Jawi Country, where the ocean has been a lifeblood for millennia. This far-flung Western Australian region is known as 'Ardi', meaning 'North East' in the Bardi language, and getting there is all part of the adventure. It's a three- to four-hour drive from Broome/Rubibi to Cape Leveque, on a sealed road that winds through rugged, sun-bleached terrain, where you can visit coastal Aboriginal communities Beagle Bay, Lombadina and Djarindjin.

Beneath the glow of those soaring rust-red cliffs, you can swim, snorkel or fish in aquamarine waters. For a deeper cultural immersion, book a Bardi-led tour, learning about the bush foods, hunting techniques and Dreaming stories of Traditional Custodians. The best time to visit is during the dry season from May to October. Permits are not required to travel on Cape Leveque Rd; however, a small access fee applies to visit the Aboriginal communities en route.

GETTING THERE

Cape Leveque is 220km (137 miles) north of Broome/Rubibi on a sealed road.

Cottesloe Beach/ Mudurup

PERTH/BOORLOO

GOLDEN SANDS DISSOLVE into the electric blue of the Indian Ocean at Cottesloe Beach – Perth/Boorloo's popular coastal playground. Hemmed by heritage-listed Norfolk Pines, 'Cott', as it's affectionately called, is known for its fiery red sunsets, sheltered turquoise waters, and the teahouse pavilion standing sentinel on its shores.

Known as Mudurup ('the place of the whiting') to its Whadjuk Noongar Traditional Custodians, who fished and held ceremonies here for centuries before colonisation, Cott's chapter as a beloved seaside retreat began in the 1880s, when the new Perth–Fremantle railway brought crowds of bathers seeking relief from the city's relentless heat.

Through the early 20th century, the beach evolved into a lively social hub, hosting festivals, concerts, pageants and even protests. This surge in popularity led to the establishment of enduring landmarks, including the Cottesloe Surf Life Saving Club, the Hotel Cottesloe (now the legendary Cottesloe Beach Hotel) and the Indiana Teahouse – all of which remain integral to the beach's identity more than a century later.

Today, Cottesloe hums with life from sunrise to sunset. At first light, ocean swimmers cut through the crisp water, their morning laps as sacred as the coffee that follows. As the day unfolds, sunbathers stretch out on the sand and kids splash in the shallows. Further out, snorkellers drift over limestone reefs, spotting silver

GETTING THERE

Cottesloe Beach is 14km (9 miles) west of Perth/Boorloo's city centre and easily reached by train. Take the Fremantle Line to Cottesloe Station, and then it's a 20-minute stroll to the beach. Buses run frequently, and parking is available but fills up on weekends.

bream, sea dragons and puffer fish; and experienced surfers carve along the reef break at Isolators. By dusk, the grassy terraces come alive with picnickers indulging in a Cottesloe ritual – a sunset plunge and fish and chips, as the sky blazes pink and gold.

With beachfront cafes and bars just steps from the sand, it's easy to spend the whole day here, dipping in and out of the Indian Ocean. The beach's accessibility and safety credentials are top-notch, with ramps and beach wheelchairs available at no cost, and lifeguards on duty on weekends and public holidays from October to March. There's also a shark net to deter curious predators. Leighton Beach, directly south, offers a wider shoreline and fewer crowds, making it a favourite for swimming, long walks and kitesurfing.

Dolly Beach

CHRISTMAS ISLAND

SOME 1500KM (932 MILES) from Western Australia, Christmas Island is known for its annual red-crab migration, which sees millions of crimson crustaceans march to their coastal breeding grounds sometime between October and January. But the remote tropical island has plenty of year-round attractions, an enviable clutch of beaches included.

Reached via a 1.8km (1-mile) trail (allow 40 minutes each way) through the otherworldly tropical rainforest of Christmas Island

National Park, Dolly Beach is a readymade Robinson Crusoe escape. An arc of ivory sand shaded by coconut palms, it has rock pools to explore, robber (coconut) crabs and nesting turtles to meet, and a dazzling fringing reef to snorkel on calm days. You can also camp here with a permit.

With no facilities at Dolly Beach, everything you bring in must also leave with you. Pay it forward to the next visitor and collect any marine debris that may have washed up.

GETTING THERE

Direct flights from Perth take three hours and 35 minutes. Flights also operate between Christmas Island and Jakarta in Indonesia (75 minutes) during the Western Australian school holidays. Dolly Beach's car park is a 30-minute drive (4WD only) from Flying Fish Cove, the island's main settlement.

Little Salmon Bay

ROTTNEST ISLAND/WADJEMUP

SLIP BENEATH THE SHIMMERING SURFACE at Little Salmon Bay, and you're in another world – a shallow reef garden where coral fans sway with the tide, colourful fish cruise in lazy schools, and the occasional octopus peeks from a rocky hideaway. Located at the southernmost tip of Rottnest Island/Wadjemup, this secluded bay is home to a marked snorkel trail, with discreet underwater information panels guiding you through a maze of marine life.

Offshore reefs create a natural swell barrier, making the bay an ideal snorkelling spot for families and beginners. Occasionally, Australian sea lions haul out on nearby rocks, and, above the water, sunbathers linger on soft white sand beneath limestone cliffs and low dunes.

The beach is unpatrolled and has no facilities, but nearby Parker Point offers public toilets and a beach access ramp. Bikes rule the roads on Rottnest Island, and the ride is part of the adventure, so clip on a helmet, follow the coastal curves and pedal your way to paradise.

GETTING THERE

Multiple daily ferries run to Rottnest Island from Fremantle/Walyalup (25 minutes), Perth/Boorloo (90 minutes) and Hillarys (45 minutes). Little Salmon Bay is 5km (3 miles) from Thomson Bay, the island's main township.

Cable Beach / Walmanyjun

BROOME/RUBIBI

A MAGNIFICENT SWEEP of blond sand caught between the turquoise waters of the Indian Ocean and the rust-red pindan soil of the Kimberley region, Cable Beach/Walmanyjun has earned its renown as Western Australia's most famous stretch of shore. Located in the former pearling port of Broome/Rubibi, the 22km (14-mile) beach is synonymous with camel trains silhouetted by blazing sunsets—a quintessential image of holidays in the northwest.

By day, swimmers wade into calm, translucent shallows, while further out, stand-up paddleboarders and kayakers glide across the bay. The northern end of the beach is open to 4WD vehicles, where locals and travellers alike set up for long, lazy afternoons. As the tide recedes, rock pools appear, inviting kids to explore, while those chasing adventure can take a Jet Ski or catamaran tour along the coast. At dusk, the sky ignites in fiery hues, and the sand becomes a stage for sunset drinks, barefoot strolls and those legendary camel rides.

For the Yawuru people, the Traditional Custodians, this coastline holds deep cultural and spiritual significance. At the southern end, Minyirr Park, a landscape of

GETTING THERE

Broome is 2000km (1243 miles) or a two-hour-40-minute flight from Perth/Boorloo. It's a 30-minute walk from the town centre to Cable Beach, or you can take a bus or taxi.

towering red dunes and coastal scrub, marks the sacred transition between land and sea. Three self-guided walking trails – Lurujarri, Minyirr and Nagula – wind through the park, each offering a different perspective on the region's Yawuru traditions, Dreaming stories and connection to Country.

Cable Beach takes its name from the undersea telegraph cable from Java that came ashore here in 1899, which was used for international communications until 1914. But Broome's ties to Southeast Asia run much deeper, with the town largely established through the pearling industry, which saw waves of Japanese, Malay and Chinese divers arrive in the late 19th and early 20th centuries. Long before commercial pearling, Aboriginal people had been collecting and trading pearl shells for thousands of years. Many were later forced into diving without protective gear, enduring perilous and often fatal conditions.

The dry season (May to October) is the best time to visit, with calm waters and balmy temperatures. Beachgoers are advised to avoid entering the water from November to April, due to the presence of deadly Irukandji jellyfish, crocodiles and sharks. Cable Beach is patrolled daily from April to October.

Monkey Mia Beach

SHARK BAY/GUTHARRAGUDA

MONKEY MIA MAY SEEM LIKE AN ODD NAME for a beach, but it's rooted in the history of this remote bay system in the Shark Bay World Heritage Area, renowned for its natural and cultural values. 'Monkey' is thought to refer to a ship that visited the area in 1834, or the colloquial term for sheep used by farmers in the former pastoral region. 'Mia', meanwhile, is an Aboriginal word for 'shelter' or 'resting place', with the remains of shellfish and marine life excavated from a cave near the beach indicating that its Malgana Traditional Custodians enjoyed many a meal here.

Monkey Mia consists of little more than a holiday park and a visitor centre fronting its namesake beach, which sweeps west from the jetty. The beach's calm, clear waters are beloved by road-tripping families, and while you won't find any monkeys here, wildlife is a key draw, with bottlenose dolphins cruising the shallows and emus patrolling the foreshore. A beach wheelchair is available and there is accessible beachfront accommodation.

GETTING THERE

Monkey Mia is 850km (528 miles) north of Perth/Boorloo, or a two-hour flight from Perth, plus a 22km (14-mile) drive from Denham (Monkey Mia) domestic airport, all on sealed roads.

Injidup Beach

YALLINGUP

IMAGINE PERCHING ON sun-warmed rocks, dipping your toes into crystal-clear waters as sea foam bubbles, churns and dances across your skin. Just add a splash of southwest sunshine and you have Injidup Natural Spa – a rock pool where the Indian Ocean's tides create a rejuvenating saltwater retreat.

Beyond the spa, Injidup Beach stretches 1.6km (1 mile) in a crescent of golden sand, flanked by towering dunes and limestone cliffs. The name Injidup comes from the Noongar word 'inji', the name of the red pea flower that grows along its cliffs. Home to three surf breaks, Injidup is a magnet for board riders, with long, powerful waves rolling in from the reef.

With strong currents and no lifeguards, Injidup Beach is recommended for strong swimmers only; however, the natural spa is a perfect, sheltered spot to get your vitamin sea. From May to October, humpback and southern right whales can be spotted breaching offshore.

GETTING THERE

Injidup Beach is a 35-minute drive (40km/25 miles) from Margaret River, which is a three-hour drive from Perth/Boorloo. The renowned Cape to Cape Trail weaves past the beach.

James Price Point/ Walmadan

BROOME/RUBIBI REGION

JAMES PRICE POINT IS one of those rare beaches where the colours don't just sing, they blaze. Its ancient cliffs smoulder in deep reds and burnt oranges, softening to swirls of pink as the headland gives way to a vast highway of pure white sand. Located north of Broome/Rubibi, this wild stretch of coast holds both prehistoric and cultural significance.

For the Goolarabooloo people, its Traditional Custodians, this land forms part of the Song Cycle, an ancient oral map guiding generations across Country. Beneath the cliffs, the exposed reef reveals 130-million-year-old dinosaur footprints, and behind the dunes, the endangered monsoon vine thickets are remnants of rainforests that covered Northern Australia millennia ago.

Visitors can camp on the beach at no charge, explore the dramatic pindan bluffs and watch as the setting sun ignites the landscape in deep reds and golds. Between June and October, humpback whales migrate past the coast. Accessible only by 4WD, James Price Point is a place where time slows, the land tells its own stories and the Kimberley's ancient spirit takes centre stage.

GETTING THERE

James Price Point is 50km (31 miles) north of Broome via Manari Rd. The journey takes 60 to 90 minutes, depending on road conditions.

Turtle Bay

DIRK HARTOG ISLAND/WIRRUWANA

REMOTE, RUGGED AND STEEPED IN HISTORY, Turtle Bay sits at the northern tip of Dirk Hartog Island – the westernmost point of mainland Australia, where the last light of the day melts into the Indian Ocean, unbroken by land for thousands of kilometres.

This is Malgana Country, though it didn't deter the navigator François de Saint-Alouarn from attempting (unsuccessfully) to claim it for France when he landed in Turtle Bay in 1772 and buried the proclamation document in a bottle.

The bay is a nesting ground for endangered loggerhead turtles. You can see them in action from October to March, but be sure to observe from a distance. Dolphins, dugongs and reef sharks can be spotted gliding through the shallows year-round. Between July and October, you might even spot humpback whales breaching over the horizon.

For the ultimate wild camping experience, pitch a tent on the low cliffs above the shore.

GETTING THERE
Situated off the Shark Bay coast, Dirk Hartog Island is accessed by barge from Steep Point. When you drive off the barge (4WD essential), it's a further 85km (53 miles) to Turtle Bay on an unsealed track.

Northern Territory

ABOVE Mindil Beach
LEFT Barinura/Little Bondi Beach

Mindil Beach

DARWIN/GARRAMILLA

BELIEVED TO HAVE BEEN NAMED after the Larrakia word 'min-deel', an edible nutgrass foraged by the Traditional Custodians of Darwin/Garramilla, Mindil Beach has long been a popular place to gather. The wide, sandy beach north of the city centre was a preferred rest area for military personnel during WWII, with one young female officer, Joyce Johnson, recalling it 'looked like Bondi', with its throngs of nurses, soldiers and aviators. A caravan park was later built on the foreshore, which has since been replaced by a casino resort and a now-famous market ground. The leafy foreshore also sets the stage for a number of festivals and events throughout the year.

Held on Thursday and Sunday evenings from late April to late October, the Mindil Beach Sunset Market is a Darwin/Garramilla institution, its food stalls the ultimate showcase of the Northern Territory capital's rich cultural diversity. Grab a steaming bowl of 'Darwin laksa', some Cypriot souvlaki, Sri Lankan roti or barbecued local seafood and join locals and fellow visitors on the sand as the sun sets across the Timor Sea in ribbons of fiery hues. Alcohol isn't sold at the market (with the exception of its Sunset Lounge; the entry fee includes exclusive seating), but you're welcome to bring your own favourite sunset tipple. You can even swim in Mindil Beach's shallow waters, with lifeguards on duty from June to September, but be aware that saltwater crocodiles could be in the water at any time, as well as deadly stingers from October to May.

3 Hour Wetland Cruise $65/$45
MARKET SPECIAL

Most visitors to Mindil Beach will be less familiar with its history as a traditional burial ground for the local Larrakia people and some of their Tiwi Islander neighbours. Following the devastating air raids on Darwin on 19 February 1942, dozens of bodies washed up on Mindil Beach were also buried here. The remains of wartime casualties were later relocated to the Adelaide River War Cemetery, south of Darwin, while bones found during the 1980s construction of the casino, on the location of the Aboriginal burial ground, were reinterred on a human-made island on Mindil Creek. The entire beach remains a significant place for local Aboriginal peoples today.

GETTING THERE

Mindil Beach is 3km (2 miles) or a 40-minute walk northwest of downtown Darwin. Shared Beam e-scooters and e-bikes can be ridden to Mindil Beach, with a Beam parking location on the foreshore.

Ngalarrkpuy/ Lonely Beach

BAWAKA, EAST ARNHEM LAND

YOLNGU CULTURE MEETS meets the teal waters of East Arnhem Land at Bawaka, a small Aboriginal community at the southern tip of the Gove Peninsula. Bawaka means 'unknown heaven', and it's an apt description for the sweep of pale sand creating a natural bridge between the mainland and a small rocky island at Ngalarrkpuy or Lonely Beach.

You'll learn on a community-run tour with Bawaka Experience (the only way to visit the beach) that Yolngu life and culture has thrived here for generations. The beach tour also includes a visit to Bungugunglu, an ancient Yolngu fish-trap dating back thousands of years.

Soak up the raw natural beauty and spirituality of this remote coastline for longer on an overnight stay at Bawaka Experience's string of beachfront cabins (or campsites) just a few kilometres from Ngalarrkpuy/Lonely Beach, with cultural experiences including spearfishing, bush cooking and weaving available to overnight guests. Swimming is permitted only under the supervision of your Yolngu hosts.

GETTING THERE

Ngalarrkpuy/Lonely Beach is 55km (34 miles) or a 1.5-hour drive south of the regional hub of Nhulunbuy. You'll need a 4WD to navigate a bush track and beach-drive towards the end of the route. Book your visit well in advance to ensure guide availability.

Galuru/East Woody Beach

**NHULUNBUY,
EAST ARNHEM LAND**

THE THIN SMILE of squeaky white sand at the north-eastern tip of the Gove Peninsula is particularly photogenic at its western end, where, on the right tide, the sand forms a land bridge to tiny Dhamitjinya/East Woody Island. Known as Galuru or East Woody Beach, this sandy strip is lapped by the sparkling Arafura Sea on one side, and the ultramarine swirl of Lombuy/Crocodile Creek on the other. But don't slip into your swimwear just yet – as the name of the creek suggests, this is a beach best suited to a leisurely stroll.

Galuru isn't only a beautiful place, but also a spiritual one, forming part of the Yolngu Dreaming (Creation story) of Wuyal, the 'Sugarbag Man', who created this remote coastal landscape in his search for *guku* or sugarbag (bush honey) made from stingless native bees.

GETTING THERE

Galuru/East Woody Beach is 5km (3 miles) from Nhulunbuy, the largest town in East Arnhem Land, via a sealed road. A visitor access permit from the Dhimurru Aboriginal Corporation is required to visit this area. You'll also need a permit from the Northern Land Council to enter East Arnhem Land by road.

Bremer Island/ Dhambaliya

EAST ARNHEM LAND

JUST OFF THE NORTHEASTERN TIP of the Aboriginal region of East Arnhem Land lies the blissfully remote Bremer Island. And at the northern tip of Bremer, called Dhambaliya by the Yolngu people in this part of East Arnhem, is a sandy cove that's unusual in northern Australia: you can swim here, in the turquoise, bath-warm Arafura Sea, safe from saltwater crocodiles. Banubanu Beach Retreat is the island's only visitor accommodation; a resort with just six comfortable tent-cabins, it keeps guests safe using technology and local know-how. The safety works both ways, too. Four of the world's seven sea-turtle species lay their eggs on Bremer's beaches between May and October, which happens to be the best time to visit the island. And there's nothing like seeing loggerhead, hawksbill, flatback or Olive Ridley turtles haul themselves up the beach at dusk, magnificently oblivious to their human onlookers.

GETTING THERE

Bremer Island can be reached by boat (40 minutes) and by air (15 minutes) from Nhulunbuy/Gove, which is an hour's flight east of Darwin/Garramilla. Permits are required to visit East Arnhem Land and can be obtained online from the Dhimurru Aboriginal Corporation (dhimurru.com.au).

Barinura/ Little Bondi Beach

EAST ARNHEM LAND

BONDI BEACH IS WORLD-FAMOUS, but are you familiar with Little Bondi? Known as Barinura to its Yolngu Traditional Custodians, it's one of several stunning beaches on East Arnhem Land's Gove Peninsula, where deep red laterite cliffs tumble into sparkling ultramarine waters. The colour contrast is particularly spectacular at the 200m (0.1-mile) cove of Little Bondi, which receives some of the region's best surfing waves. You can also camp in the dunes, and if you're lucky, you might get to enjoy this remote slice of coastal wilderness to yourself at first light. It's safest to stay out of the water during the stinger season from October to May, and look out for saltwater crocodiles year-round.

You'll need a visitor access permit (or a camping permit) from the Dhimurru Aboriginal Corporation to visit Little Bondi, as well as a permit from the Northern Land Council if you plan to drive here via the Central Arnhem Hwy; apply online.

GETTING THERE

Barinura/Little Bondi Beach is 40km (25 miles) southeast of Nhulunbuy, East Arnhem Land's largest town. You'll need a 4WD to get to the beach. With some soft-sand driving involved, and no mobile/cell reception, bringing vehicle recovery gear is a good idea.

Cobourg Coastal Camp Beach

COBOURG PENINSULA, WEST ARNHEM LAND

REACHING INTO THE ARAFURA SEA, the Cobourg Peninsula is about as wild as Australia gets. Nature rules at the tippy top of the Northern Territory's Top End, which means swimming in its tropical waters is firmly off-limits. But this multi-pronged peninsula has plenty of blissfully undeveloped beaches worth visiting for their rugged beauty.

Among them is the main beach at Cobourg Coastal Camp, a private bush camp operated by 4WD- and fishing-safari operator Venture North Safaris with special permission from the region's Arrarrkbi Traditional Custodians. The natural beauty of this thin strip of sand ramps up at sunset, when the low bauxite cliffs cradling the small cove glow with a scarlet hue. Look down from the edge and you might see baby sharks patrolling the shoreline, and you can bank on larger predators lurking beyond.

You'll need to book a tour to enjoy this beach; independent visitors will find a camping area about 25km (15.5 miles) north near Smith Point, home to its own wild beach.

GETTING THERE

Cobourg Coastal Camp is 540km (335.5 miles), or a very long day's drive northeast of Darwin/Garramilla in a 4WD. Tours include Arnhem Land permits.

Index

Image Credits

COVER: Juergen Wallstabe/Shutterstock; **2:** Emma Shaw/Lonely Planet; **6:** Ryan Chatfield; **7:** Amelie b/Shutterstock, John Crux Photography/Getty Images; **8:** Matt Munro for Lonely Planet;

PHOTOS COURTESY OF CONTRIBUTORS 10: Nicola Robb/Shutterstock; **12:** Mitchell Dann/Shutterstock; **13:** Aerometrex/500pxRF; **14:** Matt Munro for Lonely Planet; **16:** Lienka/Shutterstock; **18:** Darren Tierney/Shutterstock; **20:** Welz94/Shutterstock; **21:** Cavan Images/Alamy; **22:** Warren Chan/Shutterstock; **24:** AustralianCamera/Shutterstock; **25:** Tania Stout/Shutterstock; **27:** Mathias Berlin/Shutterstock; **29:** Nico Faramaz/Shutterstock; **30:** RugliG/Shutterstock; **31:** Nico Faramaz/Shutterstock; **32:** Peter Unger/Getty Images; **34:** Darios/Shutterstock; **36:** Martin Valigursky/Shutterstock; **39:** Juergen Wallstabe/Shutterstock; **41:** Wirestock Creators/Shutterstock; **42:** Beau Elton/Shutterstock; **44:** Emma Shaw/Lonely Planet; **45:** seanscott/Getty Images; **46:** Darren Tierney/Shutterstock; **47:** Chris de Blank/Shutterstock; **48:** David Wall/Alamy; **50:** David Wall/Alamy; **51:** ymgerman/Shutterstock; **52:** Trevor Charles Graham/Shutterstock; **53:** Travelscape Images/Alamy; **55:** Darios/Shutterstock; **56:** John Palmer, Emver Partners; **58:** Charlieiphotography/Shutterstock; **59:** Jonathan Stokes for Lonely Planet; **60:** Alex King/Unsplash; **62:** Rilla Paris/Unsplash; **63:** Jonathan Stokes for Lonely Planet; **65:** Sarah Reid; **66:** lkonya/Shutterstock; **68:** Silken Photography/Shutterstock; **70:** Ilya Genkin/Alamy; **73:** iofoto/Shutterstock; **74:** Cameron Spencer/Getty Images; **75:** Brad Quaglino/Getty Images; **77:** Jonathan Stokes for Lonely Planet; **78:** bjeayes/Getty Images; **80:** Leah-Anne Thompson/Shutterstock; **82:** Leah-Anne Thompson/Shutterstock; **85:** Aerometrex/Shutterstock; **86:** Manfred Gottschalk/Shutterstock; **87:** Wirestock Creators/Shutterstock; **88:** echoofthewaves/Shutterstock; **90:** Darren Tierney/Shutterstock; **92:** Mathias Berlin/Shutterstock; **93:** RugliG/Shutterstock; **94:** Daniela Constantinescu/Shutterstock; **95:** NickGti/Getty Images; **96:** Josh Withers/Unsplash; **99:** Mark Fitz; **100:** Mark Fitz; **101:** Manfred Gottschalk/Getty Images; **102:** kontrymphoto/Getty Images; **105:** Leah-Anne Thompson/Shutterstock; **107:** Gary Chapman/Alamy; **108:** Camila Se/Shutterstock; **109:** Amy Caccamo/Shutterstock; **110:** Wazzy/Shutterstock; **112:** Maximiliane Wagner/Shutterstock; **114:** Juergen Wallstabe/Shutterstock; **116:** S. Cleaver/Shutterstock; **117:** Ignacio Palacios/Getty Images; **118:** Adri Berger/Shutterstock; **119:** Pete Seaward for Lonely Planet; **121:** bennymarty/Getty Images; **122:** Ed Sloane/Getty Images; **123:** Chelsea Chehade/Unsplash; **124:** Serenity Snapshots AU/Shutterstock; **126:** pisaphotography/Shutterstock; **127:** Marcella Miriello/Shutterstock; **129:** WithMyEyes.DK/Shutterstock; **130:** Visual Collective/Shutterstock; **132:** cb_travel/Shutterstock; **133:** louisepogg/Shutterstock; **134:** AcropolypsePhotography/Shutterstock; **137:** Noelia Ramon/Getty Images; **139:** Robert Wyatt/Alamy; **140:** Robert Wyatt/Alamy; **141:** Henryk Sadura/Shutterstock; **142:** Greg Brave/Shutterstock; **144:** Gary Chapman/Alamy; **146:** Ivan_Yim/Shutterstock; **147:** Vicki Smith/Getty Images; **149:** Jeremy Woodhouse/Getty Images; **150:** Peter Unger/Getty Images; **151:** William Edge/Shutterstock; **152:** sg-naturephoto.com/Shutterstock; **154:** John White Photos/Getty Images; **156:** Tom Jastram/Shutterstock; **158:** Andrew Bain/Alamy; **159:** Posnov/Getty Images; **160:** Robert Wyatt/Alamy; **162:** Sarah Reid; **165:** Ziyao Xiong/Unsplash; **166:** Andrew Bain/Alamy; **169:** Tom Jastram/Shutterstock; **170:** Janelle Lugge/Shutterstock; **172:** RugliG/Shutterstock; **173:** MPIX/Shutterstock; **174:** Christopher Robin Smith Photography/Shutterstock; **176:** Andy333/Shutterstock; **177:** Emma Shaw/Lonely Planet; **178:** Joshua West; **180:** LeoPatrizi/Getty Images; **183:** Joshua West; **184:** Robert Wyatt/Alamy; **186:** Lisa Maree Williams/Getty Images; **189:** MPIX/Shutterstock; **190:** RugliG/Shutterstock; **191:** RugliG/Shutterstock; **192:** aiyoshi597/Shutterstock; **194:** kwest/Shutterstock; **197:** Ozitraveler/Shutterstock; **198:** Philip Garner/Shutterstock; **199:** Sarah Reid; **200:** Stoneography/Getty Images; **201:** Strick & Fran; **202:** Dylan Alcock/Shutterstock; **204:** Elmarie Dreyer/Shutterstock; **205:** anek.soowannaphoom/Shutterstock; **207:** larkshots/Shutterstock; **208:** John Crux Photography/Getty Images; **209:** SAPhotog/Shutterstock; **211:** paulmichaelNZ/Shutterstock; **212:** bmphotographer/Shutterstock; **214:** Ryan Chatfield; **216:** Dylan Alcock/Shutterstock; **217:** Genevieve Vallee/Alamy; **219:** lenagoesagain/Shutterstock; **220:** Jonathan Stacey/Getty Images; **222:** Tania Stout/Shutterstock; **225:** avelik/Shutterstock; **226:** Jaden Law/Shutterstock; **228:** bmphotographer/Shutterstock; **230:** Sahil Malhotray/Getty Images; **231:** bmphotographer/Shutterstock; **232:** Michael Runkel/Alamy; **233:** ZUMA Press, Inc/Alamy; **234:** Emma Jones/Alamy; **235:** David Kleyn/Alamy; **236:** Benny Marty/Shutterstock; **238:** Alex Couto/Shutterstock; **240:** Lauren Henderson/Shutterstock; **241:** Matt Deakin/Shutterstock; **242:** Lell12/Shutterstock; **244:** Wirestock/Getty Images; **247:** Lauren Henderson/Shutterstock; **248:** David Bettini Photographer; **249:** David Bettini Photographer; **250:** Andrew Bain/Alamy; **251:** dotmiller1986/Shutterstock; **253:** PhotopankPL/Shutterstock; **254:** Danita Delimont/Getty Images; **255:** aiyoshi597/Shutterstock; **257:** Mark Fitz; **258:** Mark Fitz; **260:** Mark Fitz; **262:** Mark Fitz; **265:** Sarah Reid; **266:** KennethHK/Shutterstock; **271:** paulmichaelNZ/Shutterstock;

BACK COVER: RugliG/Shutterstock

Best Beaches Australia
January 2026
Published by Lonely Planet Global Limited
CRN 554153
www.lonelyplanet.com
10 9 8 7 6 5 4 3 2 1

Printed in Malaysia
ISBN 978 18375 8763 6
© Lonely Planet 2025
© photographers as indicated 2025

Publisher & VP, Print Piers Pickard
Publisher, Gift & Illustrated Becca Hunt
Senior Editor Robin Barton
Designers Taylor Miles Hopkins, Emily Dubin
Editors Sarah Reid, Karyn Noble, Vicky Smith
Writers Sarah Reid, Louise Southerden, Rosamund Brennan, Justin Meneguzzi, Josh West
Cartographers Alexandra Murphy, Wayne Murphy
Print Production Nigel Longuet

Although the authors and Lonely Planet have taken all reasonable care in preparing this book, we make no warranty about the accuracy or completeness of its content and, to the maximum extent permitted, disclaim all liability from its use.

All rights reserved. No part of this publication may be reproduced, stored in a retrieval system or transmitted in any form by any means, electronic, mechanical, photocopying, recording or otherwise except brief extracts for the purpose of review, without the written permission of the publisher. Lonely Planet and the Lonely Planet logo are trademarks of Lonely Planet and are registered in the US patent and Trademark Office and in other countries.

STAY IN TOUCH lonelyplanet.com/contact

Lonely Planet Global Limited
Digital Depot, Roe Lane (off Thomas St),
Digital Hub, Dublin 8,
D08 TCV4
Ireland

Paper in this book is certified against the Forest Stewardship Council™ standards. FSC™ promotes environmentally responsible, socially beneficial and economically viable management of the world's forests.